PAPER INTO SCULPTURE

WI

Warne's Art and Craft Series

Paper into Sculpture

BRUCE ANGRAVE

Frederick Warne

Published by Frederick Warne (Publishers) Ltd,
London, 1981

ISBN 0 7232 2710 1
Filmset by BAS Printers Limited, Over Wallop, Hampshire
Printed in Great Britain by E T Heron & Co Ltd,
Essex and London

Contents

The Elizabethan

Introduction

I frequently find myself in the difficult position of trying to explain to a mystified audience the meaning of the words 'paper sculpture'. Having worked in the medium myself for so many years, I find it strange that most people are unaware of its existence and peculiar appeal. I hope that this book will remedy the situation.

The words 'paper' and 'sculpture' must at first seem to be strange bedfellows. Sculpture after all is arguably the noblest of the arts, whose practitioners from Praxiteles to Henry Moore have toiled and sweated through the ages at marble, wood and metal in pursuit of their elusive muse. Paper, on the other hand, is perhaps the most ephemeral and ubiquitous of mankind's inventions, originally intended to facilitate the dissemination of knowledge, but more recently much employed in the communication of unsavoury and salacious news. It is also used widely to litter the countryside and for making tickets to distribute at bus-stops. It is adopted with enthusiasm as ammunition for attacking newly-married couples and is much in demand for wrapping fish and chips. It seals otherwise convenient convenience foods effectively from the housewife's clutch and supports advertisements competitively publicising identical products. It conveys Final Demands and covers walls with often vulgar patterns. It makes exceedingly good toilet rolls.

This sorry parade must pass through the mind of my audience when they encounter the words 'paper sculpture'. Can I, they think hopefully, mean papier mâché?

Well, no. Paper sculpture is the very reverse of papier mâché. And this, I think, is where the puzzlement arises. Dictionaries define sculpture as something carved or moulded from a solid substance. And obviously you cannot 'carve' a sheet of paper, though you *can* mould it in papier mâché. Hence paper sculpture must mean papier mâché. The fact is, paper sculpture is not by definition sculpture at all. A better word would be 'constructivism'. Like architecture it is built up upon a foundation, a framework. Sub-forms are created, overlaid by outer forms through which they are glimpsed, as is the inner structure through openings in a building. Like a motor car, it is outlined air. It uses the forms—cylinders, cones, boxes—of engineering by which it is limited. It is full of tension, springs straining against anchorages. It is three-dimensional sketching, with planes for pencil marks.

Neither is paper of particular significance in paper sculpture. It happens to be a handy, relatively cheap material with just the right qualities, easily cut and manipulated. Some of the new plastics do almost as well. So do some metals.

I have often tried to analyse the appeal paper sculpture has for me. I started experimenting while still a student at art college and have continued ever since. Significantly, I have never been the least interested in the creation of sculpture in more conventional materials.

Sheer laziness you will say! And I must admit the thought of pounding away for months at a lump of marble, or slapping like a physiotherapist at sticky clay or streaming with sweat behind goggles with an oxyacetylene welder does fill me with dismay. I do sometimes wonder how anyone can remain inspired under such privation! Evidently many do, but who is to know what greater heights of inspiration they might have achieved if their lives had been a little more comfortable? Much better to snip, like me, in the dry warmth of my studio, slowly submerging myself in a sea of confetti.

But the sheer hard labour entailed when working in the traditional materials is not what concerns me so much as their tractability. For all their basic toughness, wood, stone, iron and clay can be bullied into total submission. Galatea, complete in every feminine detail, can be made, if not to step out of, at least to appear in, the marble. The fact that no modern sculptor would or could be Pygmalion is neither here nor there. The threat is everpresent.

Now this danger is entirely absent in paper sculpture. Here every form must be translated into the shapes of science, so that representationalism itself becomes a kind of abstraction. The abstraction is imposed by the material, leaving the artist free to 'communicate' as much as he likes without fear of encountering that pariah of the modern arts, naturalism. This challenge, I think, is the secret of its fascination for me. And I hope for you, too.

This book is devoted entirely to my own experience in the development of the art of paper sculpture, except for the section on historical background where I have attempted to trace some of the beginnings of the art form. Paper sculpture as we know it today is of comparatively modern origin, but the use of paper for ritualistic purposes, particularly in the Orient, goes back many hundreds of years. I touch on its use in China, Japan, Mexico, Poland and England.

The section on Materials gives as comprehensive a list as I can muster of the tools, adhesives and types of paper used in paper sculpture.

Fundamental Forms describes the basic principles upon which paper sculpture is built, and my Methods of Working is self-explanatory.

There are three exercises:

The Cockatoo—a simple exercise in the full-round and in colour.
The Cat—one of my favourite designs, also in the full-round.
The Second King—a high-relief figure originally designed (along with the other two kings) for the BBC's *Radio Times* Christmas cover some years ago.

There are also sections on portraiture, photographing, preserving and framing.

Tudor Rose for BBC television

8

Origins of Paper Sculpture

Paper, so commonplace today, was once a valuable luxury. John Evelyn, in his diary for 22 June 1664, writes:

One Tompson, a Jesuit, showed me such a collection of rarities sent from the Jesuits of Japan and China to their Order at Paris, as a present to be reserved in their repository, but brought to London by the East India ships for them, as in my life I had not seen . . . a sort of paper very broad, thin, and fine, like abortive parchment, and exquisitely polished, of an amber yellow, exceeding glorious and pretty to look on, and seeming to be like that which my Lord Verulam describes in his Nova Atlantis . . .

The invention of paper is attributed to the Chinese, and to one man in particular, Tsai-Lun, who was Minister of Agriculture to the Emperor Ho-ti in AD 105. The method of production, using, as raw materials, mulberry trees, hemp, bamboo shoots and reeds, was probably little different from that recorded by John Evelyn on 24 August 1668:

To see my Lord of St. Albans at Byfleet . . . thence to the paper mills, where I found them making a coarse white paper. They cull the rags which are linen for white paper, woollen for brown; then they stamp them in troughs to a pap, with pestles, or hammers, like the powder-mills, then put it into a vessel of water, in which they dip a frame closely wired with wire as small as a hair, and as close as a weaver's reed; on this they take up the pap, the superfluous water draining through the wire; this they dexterously turning, shake out like a pancake on a smooth board between two pieces of flannel, then press it between a great press, the flannel sucking out the moisture; then, taking it out, they ply and dry it on strings, as they dry linen in the laundry; then dip it in alum water, lastly, polish and make it up in quires. They put some gum in the water in which they macerate the rags. The mark we find on the sheets is formed in the wire.

The art of paper-making spread through the Far East, reaching Korea about AD 610 and Japan about AD 625. It reached the Arabs on the capture of Samarkand in AD 707 and was taken to India at the time of the Mohammedan invasion.

The oldest known paper in the world which can be dated was made in AD 406 and is in the Stein Collection at the British Museum in London, though there are other examples of paper which may be older but which cannot be confidently dated.

China

Although originating as a substance for writing upon, as an alternative to silk and bark, paper was early recognised as a constructional material. The Chinese adopted and adapted it for use in religious rituals, particularly those relating to the despatch of the souls of their deceased to the world of Darkness. A great deal of information is known in this connection as many of the customs were practised in China up until the end of the last century. One observer, writing in 1892, mentions puppets made of paper pasted on to bamboo splints which were placed at the feet of the dead. These puppets were known as 'feet slaves' and they were provided to act as servants to the deceased. It was also customary to make paper models of houses, furniture and other everyday possessions, including money, to be burned for the use of the dead in their afterlife. It was probably a survival from much earlier practices, when real property was thus disposed of and the paper 'feet slaves' replaced the real slaves, concubines and wives buried in the tombs of the deceased.

Another custom which survived until quite recently was the placing of a sedan chair, made of paper and bamboo, outside the house of the departed for his use on his journey. The sedan chair was fixed to the shoulders of bearers also

Jointed and coloured parchment puppet for the Chinese Shadow Theatre

made of paper, and these in turn were provided with paper money as 'advance payment' to ensure against slackness in their duties. Special shops existed for the sale of paper money for the dead, the money being packed in paper trunks, sealed with paper padlocks and put into the care of two paper puppets.

Paper flowers and other objects were also placed in the coffins. A 'paper scatterer' preceded the funeral cortège strewing paper money in front of the coffin, to tempt away evil spirits who would otherwise certainly rob the corpse. Paper lanterns were included in the procession to light the spirit on its way and a pavilion of bamboo and paper containing an effigy so horrific that all known evil spirits were certain to be paralysed with terror (a blood-red face, three eyes and a purple beard ensured that bandits were taken the same way).

Thus we see, as is so often the case, that nothing is new, and in one form or another paper sculpture has an old and long practised tradition behind it. Chinese paper dragons can be seen to this day in the heart of London, when the Soho Chinese community celebrates its New Year.

In present-day China we find, as in Poland, a vigorous revival of the ancient art of paper-cutting. Dating at least from the twelfth century AD these paper-cuts decorate the paper-covered windows in the rural districts of north and northwest China, making bright splashes of colour by day and at night turning the windows into intricate shadow silhouettes.

Both scissors and knives are employed in the production of modern Chinese paper-cuts. When scissors are used the usual practice is to cut about four at a time. When knives are used the paper is nailed down in blocks of 60 to 70 sheets and cut vertically with a variety of gouge and chisel-shaped knives. If the paper-cuts are to be coloured, watercolour dyes are floated on the top sheet so that they soak right through, tinting the whole pile. The knife-cuts are more elaborate in technique than the scissor-cuts and are often used to decorate shoes, caps, cushions, tablecloths and other household articles.

Another tradition akin to that of the paper-cuts is that of shadow theatre puppets which can be

Chinese paper-cut

traced back to the Sung dynasty and still flourish today. The figures are cut with scissors or knife from a parchment of donkey-skin. Hair, facial profiles, embroidery, leaves and ferns are all expressed in delicately cut tracery. The movable arms and legs are operated by threads from bamboo rods, exactly as are the three-dimensional puppets of the Western world, and the parchment is tinted with brilliant translucent hues which glow like coloured glass when projected by lanterns against the paper theatre screen.

Mexico

Knowledge of paper-making existed in Middle America as early as 500 AD, when the culture of the Mayas was reaching its peak. They had already built cities of stone in the jungle; their art and commerce had developed to an advanced state and the science of astronomy was well established. The Mayas had developed an elaborate system of hieroglyphic writing and this must have provided the need for a suitable substance to receive the records which their trade and discoveries necessitated. Bark was the substance used for this purpose and from it they created a paper which for fineness and durability surpassed Egyptian papyrus.

Eventually the Aztecs conquered and moved into the territories of the Mayas. In turn they adopted and continued to improve the Mayan bark paper. As with the Chinese, its constructional possibilities were soon discovered and were adopted for use in religious ritual.

A bark paper is still made today by the Sumu Indians, the method of manufacture being little different from that used by the Aztecs. The branch of a wild fig tree, 6 m (20 ft) long and approximately 30 cm (12 in) in diameter is cut and the bark peeled off in one piece. This strip of bark is soaked in water for several days, then scraped and dried in the sun. It is then soaked again and beaten over a polished log with a wooden mallet. After a few hours of this treatment the bark is transformed into thin flexible sheets called *amat*.

Information on the use of paper in ceremonial among the Mexican Aztecs comes down to us from the writing of a Franciscan monk, Bernadino de Sahagún, who taught at the Indian College of Santa Cruz in Tlaltelolco during the sixteenth century. In *History of the Things in New Spain*, he tells us that Yiacatecutli, the god of merchants, was honoured by paper offerings with which his effigies were covered. The effigy of Napatecutli, god of the rush-mat makers, was regularly adorned with a crown of black-and-white paper. In the left hand was placed a water-lily and in the right a spray of paper flowers.

Some of the stories that have come down to us from de Sahagún are nothing if not horrific. For example the gods of the waters, called Tlaloques, he tells us, were propitiated by the slaughter of children on seven mountain tops, the victims being dressed in coloured papers, a different colour for each mountain.

De Sahagún also describes how paper was used in the various monthly festivals. In the month of Toxcatl for example an image of the god Vitzilopuchli was made of dough crowned with a basket bearing a paper symbol, while young girls danced around the hearth-fires waving paper banners. The priests at this festival wore rosettes of paper on their foreheads. In the month of Etzalalqualiztli the feast of Tlaloques was held. At dawn the priests robed themselves and placed great shield shapes of paper flowers on their backs, with more paper flowers behind their heads. Paper feathers and precious stones were offered to the god at this festival, together with the hearts of the sacrificed victims, of which there always seemed to be a plentiful supply.

De Sahagún describes several other monthly festivals besides those mentioned, each involving the shedding of blood and the consumption of paper in more or less equal quantities. He also mentions the use of paper in funerary rites. The dead body, with its legs doubled up under it, was dressed in paper clothes, previously prepared by the ancients and the official paper cutters. Paper documents were placed before the body with the injunction 'See, here is with what you are to travel between two mountain ranges which are adjoining one another'. More documents exhorted it with the words 'See, here is with what you are to pass the road which is guarded by a snake'. Still more with the information, 'See, here is with what you are to pass the road over which the green lizard roams.'

When the deceased had completed his journey he was to give to Mictlantecutli, the devil, the sheaf of papers with which he had been equipped.

Mexicans in procession with paper figures

It is probable that the use of paper in modern Mexican festivals has its origin in the legends left behind by the earlier civilisations. For example, in *A Treasury of Mexican Folkways** an illustration is reproduced, with the description:

In Oaxaca City the fiesta of la Virgen de la Soledad, the Virgin of the Lonely, on the eighteenth of December, is one of the loveliest of all those celebrated in cities. She is the Patroness of the State, and the natives come to visit her from all its mountains and valleys, with gifts and sorrow-laden hearts. She is also the Patroness of the sailors who have presented her with marvellous pearls for her crown.

For several nights previous to and on the eighteenth there are calendas. These are religious processions from the various barrios, men, women and children taking part. They carry Japanese lanterns on poles, candles and some very beautiful figures of birds, a boat or some other objects wrought of flowers, leaves or coloured paper.

Great Britain

The oldest authentic example of the use of paper in Great Britain is to be found in a letter written between 1216–22. It was sent by Raymond, son of Raymond, Duke of Barbonne, to Henry III of England and therefore probably originated in France. Paper was manufactured in the south of

*By Frances Toor (Crown, New York, 1947).

France as long ago as 1189, and even at that early date was exported to England and the Low Countries.

It is believed that the earliest British paper mill was built in 1490 near Stevenage. This was the Sele Mill, owned by John Tate, son of John Tate, Lord Mayor of London. Tate's mill was visited by Henry VII in 1498 and 1499, but notwithstanding the fact that the paper was of high quality— excellent enough to be used for the 1498 edition of Chaucer (its watermark an eight-pointed star in a double circle), the mill was unable to withstand foreign competition and passed out of the family on Tate's death in 1507. Another mill was founded half a century later at Fen Ditton, and in 1588 John Spielman built a much larger mill in Dartford, Kent (its watermark a jester with cap and bells). Many more mills were erected in the seventeenth century, the first patent in Britain being applied for in 1665.

Until relatively recently paper, it must be realised, was far from being a common, everyday commodity. It was in fact all hand made until the 1850s and was, like glass for windows, a rare and valuable luxury. (Even now with modern quantity-production methods, an Imperial sheet of good hand-made paper may cost £1.00 or more.) Consequently it was never used, as today, frivolously for wrapping fish and chips, printing dreadful details of frightful murders, strikes and vice, publicising competitive but otherwise in-distinguishable products, and writing apoplectic letters to *The Times*, but prudently and with great economy and careful thought. A small boy would think twice before he made a paper boat; a little girl three times before she ventured on a paper chase. Rather she might emulate Mr Pepys's sister Pall, who on one memorable day in May sent a 'baskett . . . made by her of Paper, which hath a great deal of labour in it for countrie innocent work . . .' And so from the mists of time in the seventeenth century comes down to us, not sister Pall's paper basket, but an:

unidentified shield of arms (azure, two bars or, in chief three ascallops of the second) impaling the arms of Pyndar. The shield fashioned from silk and rolled strips

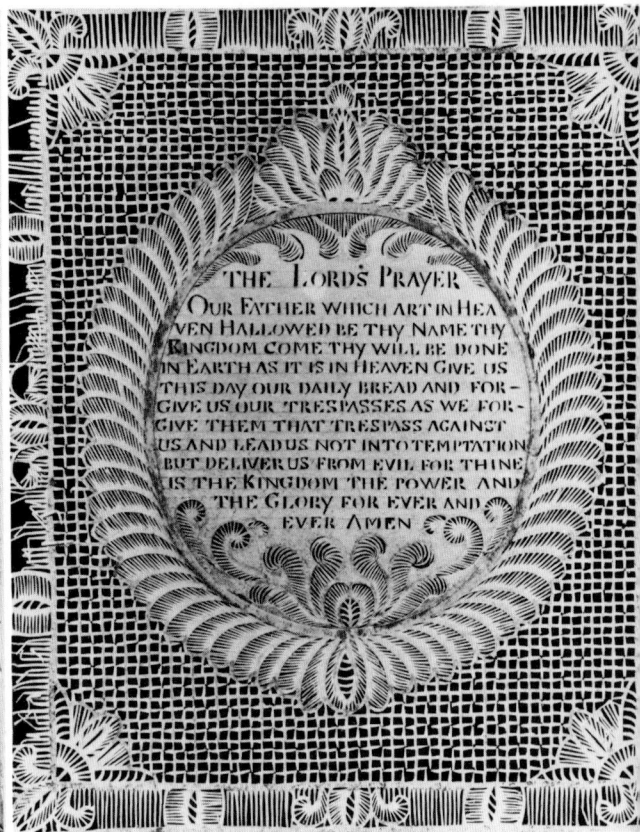

of coloured and gilded paper, surrounded by elaborate mantling and decorative borders also of rolled paper. Mounted on silk in a box frame, English, second half of Seventeenth Century. Inscribed on back Miss Mary Pyndar.

This item, which today rests at the Victoria and Albert Museum, London, was originally part of some panelling at Levant Lodge, Earls Croome. Was it made, or merely acquired, by Mary Pyndar? No one seems to know.

A great deal is known, however, of another Mary, born in 1700, a few years after the Shield of Arms was fitted into the panelling of Levant Lodge. This was Mary Delaney, daughter of Bernard Granville, who, after an unhappy first marriage, became Mrs Patrick Delaney in 1743. Mrs Delaney was something of a socialite, and not at all the type of woman, one would have thought, to take to paper-cutting in her old age, but it seems that this work absorbed all her attention for ten of the last 13 years of her life. She was about 75 when she started to make what she called her 'Paper

Mosaiks'. These had an immediate success in the fashionable world and, judging by the memoirs and correspondence of some contemporaries, were a favourite topic of conversation in her day.

Mrs Delaney devoted herself exclusively to the accurate representation of flowers and her work shows a very sound botanical knowledge. The tiniest details were meticulously interpreted in cut paper and one thousand specimens of her work are still in perfect preservation at the British Museum in London, forming an astonishing monument to her industry and artistry.

Mrs Delaney's flower mosaics were made of fine slivers of differently coloured paper painstakingly applied in layers on a black ground. Modelling and shading were all faithfully reproduced by variations in the colours, the paper being applied in layers. Veins in leaves, petals and other fine details were all separately pasted into place in the form of minute paper pieces. The only materials she ever used were paper and paste and her only tool a pair of scissors. Mrs Delaney apparently completed her

Far left *Unidentified shield inscribed 'Miss Mary Pyndar', second half 18th century (Victoria and Albert Museum, Crown Copyright)*

Left *Paper-cut by T. Hunter, 1786 (Victoria and Albert Museum, Crown Copyright)*

Below *Unidentified paper sculpture in a glazed deep frame, probably 18th century (by permission of Barbara Jones)*

thousand 'Paper Mosaiks' by 1784. In 1785 George III gave her a house at Windsor and a pension of £300 a year. She died three years later.

Close in the footsteps of the gifted and prolific Mary Delaney followed another paragon of feminine industry. This was Miss Amelia Blackburn. But there the similarity stops. For while Mary in her younger days was a fashionable and popular woman-about-court, poor Amelia spent her life quietly as a chronic invalid. And whereas the driving force behind Mary's prodigious output seems to have been the desire to record pictorially all the specimens of flora she could lay her hands on, Amelia Blackburn's work was more decorative and stylised. It was exquisite in design and

composition, as well as in technique. I quote from an article in the *Queen* of November 1911:

They are made of ordinary white kitchen paper. First the object must have been drawn very carefully, then cut out most accurately. All the details of the object, such as the petals of the flowers, the tiny feathers of the birds' wings no thicker than a hair, the fluffy tufts on their heads, were all cut out separately, each tiny cutting (some so small as to be almost invisible) being fixed in its proper place with gum. Every object is coloured and shaded accurately, according to nature, and pin pricks are used when scissors fail to get the desired effect. At first glance the impression is of a beautiful soft painting and it is only on very close examination that one can see the tiny space that divides one line from another . . .

Miss Blackburn's creations were so popular among the society of her day that they became known affectionately as 'Amelias', a name which for many years afterwards was used in reference to all paper-cuts whether or not by Miss Blackburn.

The album of Amelia Blackburn's cut paper designs at the British Museum includes some eighteenth-century work of a fineness so fantastic and microscopic in detail as to defy any attempt to imagine how it was done. This work is attributed to one Nathaniel Bermingham, of whom little seems to be known. Among the designs, in a treatment resembling wood-cutting, each stroke of modelling being faithfully perforated in the paper, are the Lord's Prayer cut in fine script on a medallion no bigger than a 5p piece and a

16

silhouette of a galleon smaller than a 1p, complete
with sails, sheets and flags, encircled by a
gossamer-like border design as thin as so many
hairs.

The creations of Mrs Delaney, Amelia Blackburn, Nathaniel Bermingham and others of their
school undoubtedly laid the foundations for the
fashion in elaborate hand-cut and later machine-
made valentines, greetings cards and other intricate lace paper-work of the mid-nineteenth
century onwards.

The story of the lace paper valentine is
remarkable enough to occupy a substantial book
on the subject by Ruth Webb Lee of the USA. The

earliest lace paper valentine was mailed on 13 February 1826 and was embossed by hand. In the 1840s and 1850s valentines of extraordinary elaboration were produced, often carrying several layers of paper lace and sometimes fascinating devices called 'cobwebs' or 'beehives' which, when activated by a silk thread, rose from the surface of the valentine like a delicate paper cage, through the bars of which could be read some sentiment, picture or verse beneath. In the 1850s mechanical valentines were marketed upon which humorous figures could be made to roll their eyes, move their arms and gesticulate vigorously to the accompaniment of a suitable verse, by pulling a paper lever at the side.

The Victorian imagination seems constantly to have been intrigued by the possibilities of paper as an educational amusement. Countless instruction books were produced with elaborate colour-lithographed diagrams, all marked, coded and prepared ready for the scissors of the rising generations in the newly erected nurseries and play rooms of the terraces in Belgravia and South Kensington.

Every evening the families would gather round the Pollock paper theatres in the withdrawing room to see the latest play (twopence coloured for Bayswater, penny plain for Pimlico), whilst Nanny and Mamma folded paper caps, boats, darts and flowers for the instruction and improvement of their young charges. Demure young ladies, otherwise elegantly unemployed, produced Papyro Plastics by the cartload for the embellishment of the neighbours' parlours, or pricked out portraits of Papa, Mamma and all their uncles and aunts 'til they pricked their fingers and fell into a swoon. At Christmas-tide ceilings groaned in sympathy with the dining tables, in their efforts to support the weight of their dependent paper swags and garlands. And every Sunday evening Papa cranked the paper discs of his Ariston organette which wheezed solemn hymns for the enhancement of the family's piety and devotion.

Opposite and above *Paper-cuts attributed to Nathaniel Bermingham (British Museum, Crown Copyright)*

Poland

A legend has grown up that modern paper sculpture originated in Poland, and is developed from the folk-art tradition of paper-cutting so well established there. Paper-cuts are of course common to many countries, often dating back for many centuries, but in Poland they seem to be particularly vigorous and varied—even though they appear to be of comparatively recent origin—as late as the seventies of the last century.

Although paper-cutting in Poland has such a short history, its origins can be traced back to much older forms of folk-art and particularly to the rich variety of folk tapestry, to mural paintings and to the decoration of furniture, such as wooden chests, very popular in peasant homes. Polish paper-cutting too owes a lot to the old techniques of leather-cutting, with designs based on those used for embroidery and lace. In recent times textile prints and wallpapers have also left their mark on the paper-cut.

The scissors used for Polish paper-cutting contain a spring which makes them particularly easy to use. These old-type scissors are still very popular in the villages and are the favourite tool of the Polish peasant women, who—like women of every other country—want their homes to look beautiful, and find that paper-cuts satisfy this desire.

Polish paper-cuts can be divided into four main groups. The first, mainly produced by the people called Kurpies, is monochromatic and geometric in composition. This type of cut is made by folding the paper twice, once longways and once across, like folding a letter to go into a square envelope. The design is then cut in such a way that, when unfolded, it is repeated in each of the four quarters, making a square or star shape (see page 21).

The second monochromatic type of cut comes from Sieradz in central Poland and is made from a single fold, resulting in a design which is symmetrical each side of a central axis. Among cuts of this kind are Leluje (trees), also called 'herbs' or 'greenery'. The main motif in such cuts is a decorative circle or oval of dense 'leaves' fringed with petals. These surround a highly stylised stem, intertwined with branches and more leaves. In the more elaborate cuts we see silhouettes of birds sitting on the branches of the main stem. The same motifs can be executed either with great wealth of complicated detail or with a directness and simplicity which makes them look as if cut in metal.

The third type, which includes cuts from the Lowicz region, features birds, and in particular cocks and peacocks, as the main theme. The designs, like the Sieradz cuts, are symmetrical, being formed out of black paper folded once. The birds are quite large relative to the rest of the design and are embellished with differently coloured layers of paper to mark combs, plumage, etc., besides flowers and leaves on the surrounding borage. (This technique of layered coloured paper closely resembles that used by Mary Delaney when she made her one thousand 'Paper Mosaics' in England during the late eighteenth century.) The tails of peacocks, for example, are quite dazzling in colour and decorative quality. On page 22 is reproduced a typical example from the Lowicz district.

The fourth and oldest type of coloured paper cut is the picture cut. This takes the form of a long strip carrying representations of scenes from the village life such as weddings, harvesting, spinning and the interiors of homes. Human characters in the cuts are always in their regional costumes.

Most paper-cutters in Poland are women, although there are men who take to it. Some cutters are true artists who often set up their own schools. As a rule paper-cutting is done direct without any drawings, though the younger generation, under school influence, do occasionally help themselves by planning their designs before cutting.

It is reasonable to deduce that all this vigorous interest in paper-cutting throughout the length and breadth of Poland led to the development of more complex three-dimensional forms and the eventual birth of modern paper sculpture. It was certainly sponsored by the Academy of Art in Warsaw and this stimulated industrial artists to use the medium for commercial purposes. Between the world wars the paper sculpture work of Polish

artists appeared in Continental exhibitions, where it began to influence English and American artists. Many brilliant Polish artists emigrated to England and America taking their talent with them. Pioneer names such as Marya Werten, Erica Hanka Gorecka and Tadeusz Lipski come immediately to mind, setting, as is so often the case among the arts, a high standard right from the outset which few have surpassed.

Above *Kurpie paper-cuts (Polish Cultural Institute)*

Below *Paper-cuts from Sieradz, central Poland (Polish Cultural Institute)*

Japan

The Japanese art of Origami can be said to be the third point of a triangle, the other two points being paper-cutting and paper sculpture. All three use paper but in entirely different ways. Paper cutting is, as its name implies, the creation of decorative art forms by perforations in a paper sheet. Paper sculpture is built up three-dimensionally from shapes cut and glued together. Origami, on the other hand, is pure paper-folding, starting from a square or rectangle of paper and ending as one of hundreds of different figures, from butterflies to brontosauri.

A Japanese friend of mine—a professor at Kyoto University—visited me recently and during dinner in a local restaurant created a Flying Crane out of the menu card. He told me that during the many conferences he attends he invariably 'doodles' Origami and slowly disappears behind a mountain of frogs, tortoises, cranes and fishes. These creatures in particular belong to the old tradition of Origami in Japan, symbolizing good luck, long life, aspiration, love and fertility.

If, as a child, you have ever made a paper cap, boat or dart you have practised Origami. You are in distinguished company for both Percy Bysshe Shelley and Charles Dodgson (the Lewis Carroll of *Alice in Wonderland*) were keen Origamists.

Many books are available on the subject, including *The Art of Origami* by Samuel Randlett (Faber) and *Origami 1*, *Origami 2* and *Origami 3* by Robert Harbin (Coronet).

23

My Own Experience

When I was a student just before World War II the graphic art of communication had reached a high level of sophistication in Western Europe. The best press advertising, London Transport posters, *Vogue* and *New Yorker* covers, all inspired by the recently demised but freshly remembered activities of the Bauhaus with its spawn of abstract art and modern architecture, seemed to be pointing the way to new heights of achievement.

Marvellous advertising campaigns by Shell and Guinness, striking posters by McKnight Kauffer, Rex Whistler, Austin Cooper, Lewitt-Him and Eckersley-Lombers, astonishing theatre designs by Erté—all faithfully reported by that bible of the art communicators *Gebrauchsgraphik*—filled us students with the conviction that we were the rightful inheritors of the whole historical tradition of Art. Art, we reasoned, had always been for communication and we were the 'New Communicators'.

The Sphinx

Gebrauchsgraphik, an international art periodical published in Germany, appeared regularly with all that was best in the new world of the Art Communicators. And one day it appeared with a feature on the paper sculpture of two artists, Kallister and Dronsfield. As I recall, Edi Kallister had designed a series of sculpture heads like theatre masks, and Dronsfield a pill-box hatted Ruritanian soldier aggressively brandishing a fixed bayonet over a palisade.

Dronsfield's Ruritanian astonished me with its vitality and the more astonishing fact that it was made of paper. Its appeal was immediate and it set me to work at once on my own experiments.

So it was the work of Dronsfield and Kallister which first started me off on paper sculpture. I made several early constructions, including a Lord Mayor and a Sphinx, with varying degrees of success. The Lord Mayor's chain was made of pieces of paper doilies and the Sphinx was half-buried in real sand. But I quickly became a purist and am now so averse to trick effects that I use for preference only one make of paper for my work and certainly no doilies.

I first encountered really advanced examples of paper sculpture when visiting the New York World's Fair in 1939. Within the Polish pavilion as I recall were some elegant, decorative and beautifully constructed heraldic eagles. I still remember the excitement I experienced on seeing them for the first time.

During the war I worked with the Ministry of Information and in my free time experimented with portrait sculptures, photographs of which appeared in several British publications. I made about 30 sculptures of various VIPs from Neville Chamberlain to Joseph Stalin. These full-round portrait sculptures were very complex and many were the headaches accompanying their design and construction. But they taught me a lot about

The Cow that Swayed in the Wind

the techniques needed for the mastering of this odd and unfamiliar medium.

As I became more skilled in the designing of these sculptures I developed a method of interlocking the paper so that eventually it became possible for me to construct the portraits without any adhesives at all. I patented this method of construction in Britain, America and Canada and a short film was made of it by Pathé during the 1940s.

One of my first commercial constructions at the end of the war was The Cow that Swayed in the Wind, a disconsolate creature ready to flap like a flag in the slightest gust, so great was its need for the cattle fodder marketed by the company which commissioned it. Then came The Lovers and the Town Crier, commissioned by Columbia.

In 1946 I found myself placed suddenly on the international map by a sixteen-page review in the Swiss art journal *Graphis*, followed by others in the French *Publimondial* and the British *Display*. These reviews started a kind of 'reputation snowball'; I suddenly found myself working hard and almost continuously producing paper sculptures for advertisements and exhibitions. There was a series of eight or ten figures for the Odhams *Woman* stand at the Ideal Home Exhibition; a large sculpture of Prince Charming trying the glass slipper on Cinderella for a long-forgotten client; two small Puritans in full-round for Lintas; a

poster showing a Butler rapidly transporting a bottle of Seagers Gin to a parched and grateful Employer; and, among many others, a Cockerel in paper sculpture perched on a Pathé Pictures weathervane. The central T of Pathé was common to the two words which formed a cross pointing to the four corners of the earth. The device was to appear to be floating in the sky without support. To achieve this I embarked on an experiment in *trompe-l'œil*, the whole composition, including paper sculpture, being mounted on a sheet of plate glass. The lettering was drawn in false perspective on the flat glass plane.

During 1949 the monthly magazine *London Opinion* asked me if I could produce a series of covers in full-colour paper sculpture. The theme was to be similar to one that had adorned the cover of the American magazine *Esquire* for some time—an elderly but virile gentleman's attempt to undo the virtue of a beautiful but chaste maiden. As far as I can remember the *Esquire* covers were reproduced from figures made of modelling clay or Plasticine. My paper sculpture gentleman was a dapper English type, usually in a top hat and with a tendency to twirl moustachios. The girl's evident desire not to succumb showed, one felt, considerable lack of judgment. Those, after all, were the days before mods, rockers, teds, punks, muggers

Opposite *The Town Crier*

Below *Symbol for Pathé Pictures*

and pop and one felt she had little to fear.

At about this time the Festival of Britain dawned on the horizon. I designed the decorations for various parts of this, including the Tree Walk with its 12 m (40 ft) Dragon in the Festival Gardens and a set of 20 paper sculpture figures for the Outdoor Sports and Games Section in the Land Traveller Exhibition—a kind of touring Festival of Britain, roaming round the larger cities of the country.

It always seems to rain when delivering paper sculptures and this can present a hazard as paper stretches when damp. Once I drove to Stoke-on-Trent with a cargo destined for a pottery exhi-

bition. The sculptures depicted workmen operating stylised versions of pottery-making machinery, much of which was made of flat-sided box forms. About four inches of rain fell during the journey with the result that interesting blisters appeared in the originally crisp-looking structures. Though these began to fade under the warm lights of the exhibition they added their quota of anguish to an already exhausting episode.

My contribution to the Coronation was a pair of sculptures for the Craft Centre of Great Britain, then stationed in Hay Hill. These figures were the first sculptures salvaged at the end of their 'commercial life' and one of them, cleaned and renovated, is now the oldest specimen in my collection of about 50 sculptures. At the time of writing, this one—of an Elizabethan man in ruff and breeches—is 25 years old and still, in its glazed deep-frame, as fresh as when renovated late in 1953. From then on I tried to recover my sculptures at the end of their commissioned life, though many were lost and now exist only as photographs. Among these were an elaborate Crest for Seagrams and two 1926-type flapper girls charlestoning, in full colour, for the foyer of the Beachcomber restaurant in Mayfair.

The steady flow of commissions continued throughout the 1950s, including some of comparatively enormous size. On these occasions my house and life tend to become entirely dominated for the duration of the commission. The first example of complete domination occurred when I was living packed into a very small flat near Baker Street. It was also my first essay in metal sculpture—two 2·7 m (9 ft) horses (one a seahorse with a fish tail) for Ruston and Hornsby, made in nickel-silver. Maquettes for these (still in my collection) were made in paper first, the shape of each structural unit being preserved on tracing paper as it was designed. Subsequently all the shapes were photographically enlarged to the correct scale for the finished sculpture. The paper bearing the enlarged shapes was then stuck with rubber gum on to the metal sheet, which was in turn cut out with shears, backed with microply and assembled

Opposite *Paper sculpture for a commercial poster (photographs of a real bottle and glass, etc, were added to the tray)*

Below *Old and Modern Golf. For the Festival of Britain, Land Traveller Exposition*

on armatures of 12 mm ($\frac{1}{2}$ in) plywood. I well remember soldering the units of the tail over the flame of my gas cooker.

The Three Kings was commissioned by the BBC for use as a cover design of the Christmas *Radio Times* and subsequently for a window display at Broadcasting House. It also featured later in an exhibition of *Radio Times* drawings held at a gallery in Piccadilly. Accompanying the framed sculpture was a similar frame showing the working diagrams of The Second King. These are reproduced in this book together with step-by-step photographs of the construction sequence.

On another Christmas occasion I designed a group of reindeer towing a sleigh bearing Santa Claus with his sack for the window of the *Daily Mirror* building in Holborn. The figures were almost life size but were eclipsed the following year by a set of sculptures each over 2.5m (9 ft) high to decorate a New Year's Eve Ball at the Albert Hall. In every case these large-scale figures were designed as small maquettes first.

Many of my sculptures are in high relief—half sculptures in fact—designed to be seen only from the front. This is because so many of them are made for photography or for display upon the wall

Opposite *Crest for the House of Seagram*

Above *Sea Horse (2·7 m wide) in metal sculpture from a paper sculpture maquette. For an industrial exhibition*

or background of an exhibition structure. The four sculptures for Marley floor coverings made an interesting change, being in the full-round. Three of these, a Gondola with Gondolier, a Chariot with two Chargers and a Charioteer, and the Leaning Tower of Pisa, were rescued, the Chariot with two Chargers appearing in this book.

Every few years a particularly exciting commission comes my way. In the mid-sixties James Gardner, whom I had known from the Festival of Britain days and earlier, was working on the internal design of the fantastic Evoluon Museum at Eindhoven in Holland—a stupendous flying saucer on stilts hovering in front of Philips

Electrical Industries. I was commissioned to produce two sets of five 'stages', all in paper sculpture. The first set showed incidents from 'A Day in the Life of an Eighteenth Century Aristocrat'. The sculptures, in white and on a small scale but with considerable detail, were set against formalised and strongly coloured backgrounds. The second set, in full colour, represented 'A Day in the Life of a Fourteenth Century Peasant'— 'Getting Up', 'Adam Delves', 'Eve Spins', 'Feeding', and 'Sleeping'. These structures were all animated by electric motors. 'Getting Up' showed Adam stretching and yawning while Eve scratched herself. 'Adam Delves' depicted Adam

31

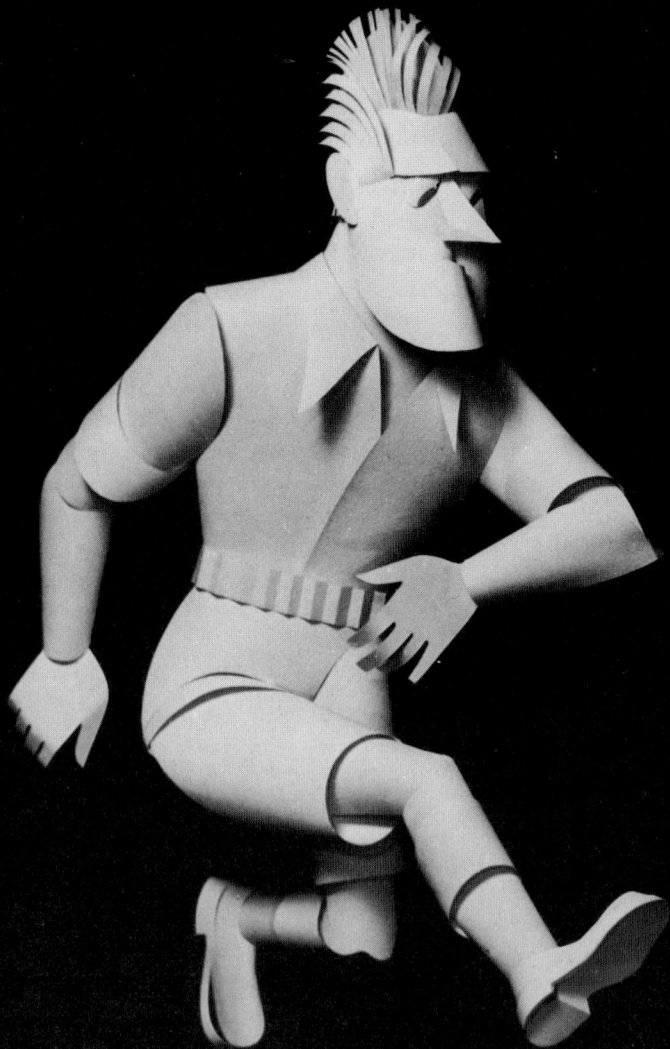

Above *The Footballer and the Cricketer (W. G. Grace)*

Opposite *The Pop Singer, for the Spirit of Youth Ball, Royal Albert Hall*

working away with his hoe; 'Eve Spins' portrayed his wife treadling her spinning wheel, whilst rocking the cradle with her other foot; 'Feeding' revealed Adam and Eve shovelling food into their mouths and 'Sleeping' found both of them in bed, the counterpane of which heaved rhythmically to their breathing.

Towards the end of the sixties I designed a poster for Trumans Beer depicting Captain Cook and a Spaceman seated each side of the Truman 'T'.

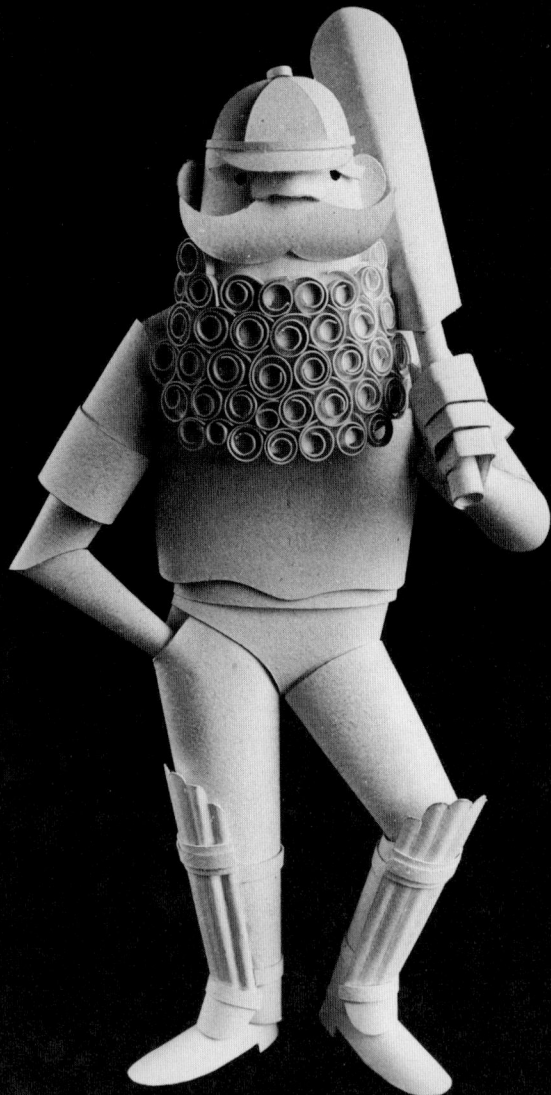

This was to coincide with the great era of American Moon landings. During May 1969 I constructed two full-round paper sculpture Magpies feathering their paper sculpture nest with jewels 'pinched' from Mappin and Webb. The trinkets were put in afterwards by the advertising agency. As always, finding a suitable reference when one needs it proved almost impossible but I finally finished up in a very secret part of the Natural History Museum, inspecting a rather battered and with-

Left *'Flapper-girl' figures (1.5 m high) for a Mayfair restaurant*

Opposite *Two examples from a series of cover designs for* London Opinion

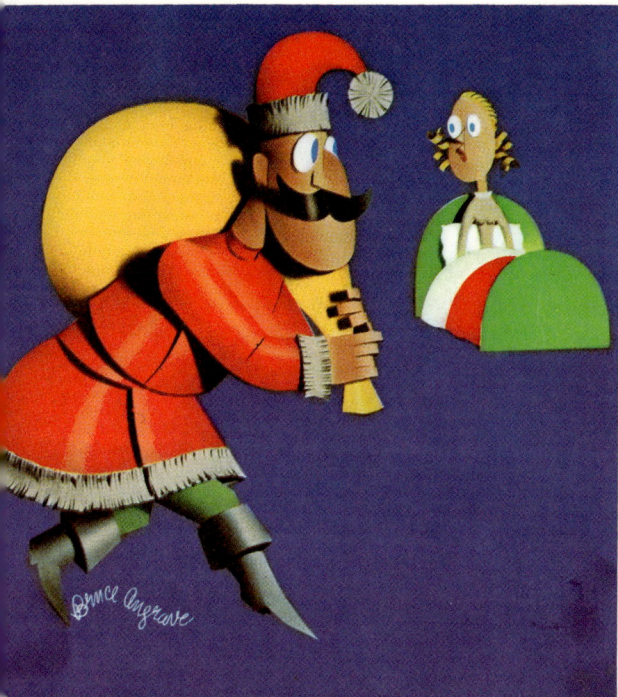

ered looking magpie's wing, before I found out what the underneath part looked like.

In June of 1969 I started work on part of the British Pavilion for the International Exposition—Expo 70—at Osaka, Japan, which was to open the following March. I was commissioned to design several sections in paper sculpture including an interpretation of Drury Lane Theatre. This was over 1 m (3 ft) wide and 2 m (6 ft) from front to back. Another section was the Nash Terrace in Regent's Park called Park Crescent—over $2\frac{1}{2}$ m (9 ft) across. Neither of these offered a lot of scope for creative imagination, being accurate though formalised representations of existing buildings—though the Nash Terrace gave me cause for concern when my cat got inside and began to peer anxiously through the windows. Shakespeare's Globe Theatre of 1612 offered more scope, as so little is known of the original. My version was taken from a print of 1812 which was based on a drawing made in Shakespeare's time. Finally there was a carousel or merry-go-round, 2 m (6 ft)

across, revolving twice per minute and carrying eight stages, each containing well-known scenes from plays, representing the English theatre from Shakespeare to John Osborne.

This Expo 70 commission was another occasion when my house and life became dominated by paper sculpture. The grand piano was totally submerged by Park Crescent; my dining table became a platform for the revolving carousel; Drury Lane Theatre dominated the sitting-room floor; and Shakespeare's Globe filled most of the studio. The eight theatre stages were dotted about the rest of the house. When completed in February 1970 these were all flown out to Osaka and as befits a dedicated and concientious artist, I flew myself out to Japan after them so that I could supervise their installation.

The Expo 70 commission was, I think, the largest I have ever done, but at least I had seven or eight months to complete it. But the biggest take-over of all occurred early in 1972. I was asked by the Central Office of Information to construct six stages of life-size animated paper sculptures plus 68 colour drawings for the Ministry of the Environment stand at the Ideal Home Exhibition. I had eight weeks to complete this marathon and the period coincided with the 'Great Power Cuts'. I was moving house at the time and the power cuts occurred at different times in each house, so I spent many hours driving helter skelter from one house to the other in order to take advantage of the available electricity. Fortunately I found an excellent firm of animators in Putney (working on yet another power-cut schedule) and the following six weeks were the most strenuous I have ever spent. Meanwhile both houses became filled with life-size paper sculpture figures of architects, grandmas, parrots, retired gentlefolk, beer drinkers, cleaning ladies and a scratching dog, all animated by electric motors.

At about this time I designed three large and elegant Cockades for the Lafayette restaurant in St James's. But perhaps the most elegant commission I have ever done came from the designers of the motor vessel *Eagle*, a car ferry cum small cruise liner which was to ply between Southampton, Lisbon and Tangiers. It was a beautifully fitted-out ship, rather like a miniature QE2, and the problem was the creation of glittering Eagle symbols in metal, one for the reception area and the other to be mounted behind the Captain's table in the restaurant. I solved the problem by constructing the symbols in metal foil after designing the maquettes in paper first. The metal foil Eagles were then encapsulated in solid perspex discs about 1 m (3 ft) in diameter and 6 cm (2 in) thick. This highly experimental encapsulation was done superbly by some plastics wizards in south London. One of the problems attendant upon this commission arose from the mechanical stresses in the perspex during

Opposite *The Gendarme and The Little Mermaid of Copenhagen, for a paper manufacturer*

Above *Roman Chariot, a full-round paper sculpture for a floor tile manufacturer*

encapsulation. As the material sets around the sculpture, immense pressures in the region of tonnes to the square centimetre are brought to bear upon it by shrinkage. To avoid the sculpture being crushed it had to be made with no armature supports and no pockets where air could be trapped.

The Little Mermaid of Copenhagen and The Gendarme, each designed for a firm of paper manufacturers, were interesting essays in the almost full-round. As always, the human form proved the most exacting test of an artist's skill and the Little Mermaid, with her feminine curves, provided a headachey exercise in translation to the cylinders and cones of paper sculpture. Spicer's

Penguin, on the other hand, lent itself easily to formalisation, emerging quickly as a figure in the full-round.

One of the most difficult commissions ever offered me was for a pair of sculptures, each 2 m (6½ ft) tall, of the British Lion and the Berlin Bear, intended for the front façade of an inn to be erected for British Week in Berlin. The commission had to be completed within eight weeks without disrupting my normal everyday flow of work. To save as much time as possible I decided to dispense with the usual small-scale maquettes, working direct on the full-size sculpture. Accordingly I made small-scale working drawings first and then enlarged them to full size, gradually covering the

Above *The Way of the World*

Below *Pygmalion*

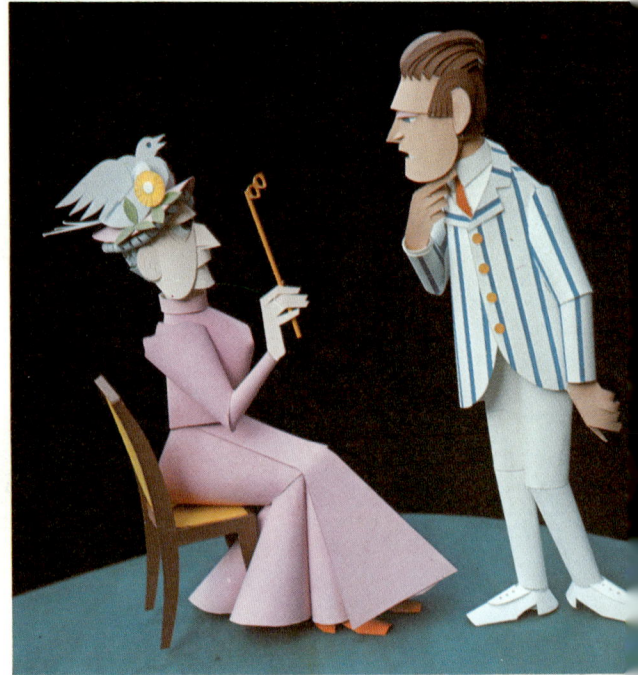

Above *The Importance of Being Earnest*

Above *The School for Scandal*

Below *Private Lives*

Above *Iolanthe*

floors of the studio and sitting-room with pasted-together sheets of tracing paper covered with squares. The full-size working drawings were so large that they had to be divided into parts and keyed together at the junctions as I needed them. The armatures were made of 12 mm ($\frac{1}{2}$ in) plywood, cut to shape with an electric jigsaw in the garage, while my car made the best of the winter outside. Before I could begin to work on the finished sculptures these armatures had to be set up on gantries of timber formed from two triangular end supports 2·5 m (8 ft) high with rectangular frames 2 m (6 ft) square set between them and pivoted at the centre. The armatures were suspended within the frames on wires. The pivots enabled the frames to be swung forwards and backwards along with the armatures so that I could work on awkward parts of the sculptures without crawling on the floor or hanging from the chandelier. As these structures were set up in my drawing room, all thoughts of social activity were abandoned.

But if the Lion and the Bear were amongst my most difficult assignments, by far the most complex was the poster for London Transport. This comprised an almost full-round figure of Sir Christopher Wren in full colour and dressed in the style of about 1700, posing with his walking cane and sword before a montage of his towers, six in all, fronted by the central dome of St Paul's Cathedral and part of the side elevation. In the foreground were two small pedimented structures bearing this legend, modestly composed by myself:

> Sir Christopher Wren
> Took up his pen
> And Worked for Hours
> On the City Towers
>
> You can visit them Still
> Without any Fuss
> By London Transport
> Train or Bus.

The Wren poster was under construction for about 18 months, entirely because London Transport was quite willing to wait for as long as I wanted and as a result the thing became an exercise in complexity. Fortunately it is still in my possession and now resides in my exhibition room.

In the mid-sixties I was invited to hold an exhibition of paper sculpture at the showrooms of

Opposite *The Berlin Bear and The British Lion, for a British Week exhibition in Berlin*

Above *The Globe Theatre of 1612, for Expo 70, Osaka, Japan*

the Reed Paper Group in Piccadilly. This was so successful that its run was extended and I was afterwards commissioned to design a portrait head of Cecil Harmsworth King, chairman of the company. So many sculptures were being commissioned at this time that it is impossible to recall them all. There was an animated sculpture of an early nineteenth-century maiden cranking a barrel-organ for a BBC TV production called 'Take a Note'; a set of life-size sculptures for the fashion pages of *Woman* and subsequent window display at Swan and Edgar's; a crest for Embassy cigarettes; and three 'Gonks' for EMI. At this time I also designed the Cat, as a personal gift to the editor of *Woman*.

In the mid-seventies the *Financial Times* asked me to design paper sculpture figures for their theatre programme advertising. The subjects had to include actual *Financial Times* newsprint (pink in colour). The subjects chosen were a scene from the opera *Il Seraglio*, another from the ballet *Petrushka*, and an eighteenth-century musician playing the harpsichord. The pink newsprint was used for the prosceniums and curtains, the figures being in bright colour.

Finally, my latest commission at the time of writing has been a kind of fantastic city for Letraset, using as many of their products—coloured papers, transfer lettering and decorations, markers and aerosols—as possible. I was lucky here. It did not invade my house, but a friend's cottage instead!

41

Requiem Canticles
by CLEMENT CRISP
Figaro
Arts news in brief
Elizabeth Hall
Segal & Kalichstein
GRIFFITHS
by DOMINIC
Donald Swann
by B. A. YOUNG
Cosi fan tutte
Giselle
The Ring
L'Africaine
by ANDREW PORTER

Opposite *Il Seraglio and* above *The Harpsichordist, for the* Financial Times

Methods of Working

Most of my paper sculptures are commissioned for commercial purposes, such as window display, and for the embellishment of commercial or prestige expositions. Also for publicity in one form or another or for illustration. These last use the sculptures in the form of photographs in colour or black and white.

I have found that, for most such purposes, sculptures in high relief, designed to be seen from one position only and mounted in front of a suitable background, are easier to design and construct than full-round sculptures. They are also more securely under my authority as designer, as I have full control over the background and the exact angle of view. Both these details are as important as the sculpture itself in achieving the correct effect.

Preliminary sketches

Let us suppose that I have been commissioned to design a paper sculpture figure in high relief, in colour, on a background. I start by experimenting with pencil scribbles. These sketches are quite small, usually about 8 cm (3 in) high or so. While experimenting, I keep constantly in mind the fact that the sculpture is to be in high relief, with foreshortened front-to-rear dimensions. These distortions impose considerable limitations on the design, but as a result of experience I find I subconsciously allow for this, instinctively planning the figure to take advantage of the limitations imposed by high relief in the arrangement of limbs, posture, facial construction and general silhouette.

The working drawing

After I have planned the sculpture to my satisfaction (and perhaps shown my sketches to the client at this stage so that he has some idea of my intentions) I then 'develop' it into idiomatic paper sculptural forms—redrawing through detail paper until I have evolved a satisfactory perspective diagram showing how the finished sculpture will look. The facility for doing this comes easily with experience. I often experiment with several different designs at this stage, deciding thereby at the outset exactly how the sculpture is to be constructed. I usually leave almost nothing to chance on the actual construction, and the final working diagram is almost identical to the form the sculpture will take when it is completed.

This working diagram is very finely pencilled, like a draughtsman's plan. I like to use continuous-feed repeater pencils such as the Parker automatic with Writefine B leads. These are about half the thickness of those used in ordinary propelling pencils and do not need constant pointing. Furthermore the leads are gripped firmly by the repeater mechanism and do not move loosely within the nozzle as is so often irritatingly the case with ordinary propelling pencils. Like so many specialised things, such as the lamented Whatman drawing paper, these Parker repeater pencils have for some time been discontinued by the makers. However, new continuous feed pencils, which appear to be efficient, have recently been introduced by Parker, Rotring and various other makers.

The finished working diagram (still a miniature about 8 cm (3 in) or so high but now on tracing paper) is then fitted into the plate carrier of my photographic enlarger between two pieces of glass and projected to form an enlarged image the same size as the intended sculpture. This image is carefully traced on to detail paper and serves as the master diagram.

Above *Park Crescent, Regent's Park, London (3 m wide), for Expo 70, Osaka, Japan*

The armature

Next I design the sculpture's armature. 'Armature' is simply a technical name for any load-bearing structure within a sculpture to give it stability and support. All my high-relief constructions are built on armatures which take over the load-bearing duties of the paper, leaving it free to do its job of expressing form. I used to use plastic laminated sheet and sometimes aluminium for this, but, although I still use metal when the armature is particularly slender or needs to take up more than one plane, I now prefer a miraculous substance called microply, which is a three-ply wood laminate about $1\frac{1}{2}$ mm ($\frac{1}{16}$ in) thick or less. Microply of the right thickness is very flexible in one direction and quite rigid in the other. Furthermore it can be cut as easily as paper with strong scissors or metal shears. Hence the drudgery of profiling the armature with a jig or fretsaw is eliminated. Two layers of microply, Uhu-ed or Bostik-ed together with the grain at right-angles, make a remarkably rigid though thin and light structure. Alternatively the microply can be stiffened where necessary with balsa wood strutting.

Laying another sheet of detail paper over the master diagram, I plan out the shapes of this armature by drawing a very much simplified outline of the intended sculpture about 3 or 5 mm ($\frac{1}{8}$ or $\frac{1}{5}$ in) (according to scale) within the boundaries of the master diagram. When the sculpture is put together the attachment points or tabs of its various parts will be lapped over the edges of this armature and secured at the back with the impact adhesive. Some parts of the armature, for example head parts and limbs, which may lie in a different plane from the main body of

the sculpture, are made up as separate units. I used to fix these parts with threaded studding or bolts which, combined with nuts, acted as distance pieces governing the relative angle of the planes. By adjusting the nuts the angle could be varied until the right effect was achieved. Since changing over to microply, however, and also to impact adhesive which is so much stronger than the adhesives I used previously, I find it more convenient to cut wedge-shaped pieces of balsa wood and simply glue the different planes into place. Balsa wood is usually adequate for these spacers.

When I need an armature part, the whole of which does not lie in the same plane, such as a leg bent at the knee and projecting forward from the main body of the sculpture, I sometimes use aluminium sheet. This is quite easy to cut and is readily bent to shape. It can also be stiffened where necessary with strips of wood glued into place. I fix these aluminium parts in position with screws or bolts.

When I use aluminium instead of microply the problem of transferring the armature shapes to the shiny metal has to be tackled. This is easily done by sticking the detail paper carrying the drawing of the shape directly on to the aluminium with rubber gum. The drawing and underlying metal can then be cut out simultaneously with shears. The advantage of using rubber gum for this purpose is that the paper can be pulled off easily after cutting and the dry rubber gum cleaned off with a finger.

When the shapes of all these armature parts have been designed I trace them down on to microply and cut them out with strong scissors or shears. The best shears for the purpose are those shaped like scissors, with thumb and finger holes,

SIR CHRISTOPHER
WREN
TOOK UP HIS PEN
AND WORKED
FOR HOURS
ON THE CITY TOWERS

YOU CAN
VISIT THEM STILL
WITHOUT ANY FUSS
BY
LONDON TRANSPORT
TRAIN OR BUS

Opposite *Sir Christopher Wren, a poster for London Transport*
Above *The Peacock (1.5 m high) in full-round paper sculpture painted in acrylic colours, for an exhibition in Nigeria*

The Stag

rather than the kind resembling secateurs. When handling microply it is as well to remember that it cuts very easily in one direction but is inclined to split in the other, due to its inherent one-way rigidity and consequent stiffness under the shears. For this reason when using shears I try to avoid the coincidence of long straight lines on the armature with the grain of the wood. On the other hand, as the microply is naturally rigid in one direction it is useful to take advantage of this quality, for example in the case of an arm, where the grain should run longways to give it stiffness without the need for strutting. Such straight lines along the grain in microply can be easily cut with a scalpel and straightedge on the glass cutting sheet.

Naturally, if the sculpture is to be larger than a certain size, say 1 m (3 ft) high, microply will not be rigid enough to support its parts. Then I resort to ordinary plywood of any thickness up to 12 mm ($\frac{1}{2}$ in) depending on the scale of the finished construction. Such material is much too tough for shears, and is best dealt with by a hand-held electric jigsaw. This will rip through thick plywood with great speed and can follow quite sharp curves without difficulty.

When I have cut out all the armature parts, I drill any bolt holes that may be needed, including the two or more in the main armature unit to accommodate the long bolts which will eventually attach the sculpture to its background. These support bolts will be gripped rigidly in their holes with nuts screwed right up on the reverse side of the armature. More nuts will be screwed on to the bolts when the sculpture is finished, to govern its distance in front of the background. The ends of the bolts which project through the background will then be secured by still more nuts and the whole sculpture thus be rigidly mounted. An alternative method is to use blocks of wood directly glued on to the back of the sculpture after it is finished, and secured through holes in the background by screws. The bolt method allows for finer adjustment, but the wood block mounting is probably simpler.

The paper sculpture itself

I now assemble the various parts of the armature and can, at last, get on to the next stage, the construction of the paper sculpture itself. In the case of a human or animal figure I usually start with the head as I find, in paper sculpture as in drawing, that a successfully designed head influences the approach to the whole of the rest of the figure. The head, too, is often a fairly complicated piece of construction and the successful solution of this problem inspires one to make shorter work of the rest of the figure.

I am not going to give here a list of step-by-step rules on how to make heads, bodies, arms and legs. I look on paper sculpture as a legitimate art form, and feel that every artist working in the medium should develop his own techniques and give full play to his own creative powers. I do give full details of three exercises (see pages 66–89), but the purpose of this book is primarily to show you what *I* do, and to leave you to draw your own conclusions and improve on my technique.

For example, I find it best to keep the basic forms simple, in keeping with the limitations of the medium—forms that can be made from cones, cylinders and folds. This is just one way of course. Other artists adopt an altogether freer approach, and doubtless you will evolve an entirely different technique again. But my way is to keep the basic structure as simple as I can, and to add interest (depending on scale and degree of detail envisaged

at the outset) in the treatment of surface units, hair, eyes, lips, etc. Everything has to comply with the 'legitimate' use of stiff paper—no crumpling, moulding, doilies, real buttons or chain-store trinkets. But that is just *my* way; I have no right to stop you using the Hope diamond if you insist!

However, although I do not want to lay down any rules for the designing of heads and other parts, my method of turning the sketched units on the master diagram into paper units on the paper sculpture is a process of technique rather than style, and it will be generally helpful to the student to describe it in some detail.

In the case of a head of a typical 1 m (3 ft) figure, such as the Elizabethan (see pages 64–5), the main unit may consist of a single piece forming the mask of the face, the ears and part of the hair. I pencil a line down the centre of the face in the master diagram and then lay over it a piece of detail paper. On to this I trace the centre line. Next I trace off the outlines of the mask for a distance of about 3 cm (1 in) on each side of the centre line. The tracing is then moved about 1 cm ($\frac{1}{3}$ in) to the right and the *left-hand* part of the mask is completed to the edge of the master drawing. The top and bottom lines of the mask are then extended for about 5 cm (2 in) beyond the edge of the master drawing, to form a mounting tab. I repeat the process on the right-hand part of the mask by moving the tracing 3 cm (1 in) to the *left* of the centre line at the corresponding point in the process.

This complicated-seeming but really quite straightforward procedure is adopted to 'spread' the mask enough to allow for its representation in high relief on the paper sculpture, and the method is applied to all the parts on the master diagram which are to be similarly interpreted in high relief. Experience soon enables you to judge how much to 'spread' each part. The general rule is the wider the spread the higher the relief produced.

When I have finished 'spreading' the mask on detail paper, as described above, I turn it over and rub the diagram down with the blade of a curved kitchen knife on to a piece of suitable construction paper. The pencil image is thus transferred in reverse to the paper, and can be cut out with the scalpel on the glass cutting sheet. This method has

Opposite *Eagle symbol in metal foil encapsulated in solid perspex (1 m diameter)*
from paper sculpture maquette, for the motor vessel Eagle
Above *Magpies in full-round paper sculpture, for a jewellery brochure*

two advantages. Firstly, only one pencilling process is necessary and the tracing is transferred accurately by mechanical rubbing, and secondly the pencil marks are on the *back* of the paper, which does not therefore have to be cleaned up after cutting.

After this I apply a cylindrical 'bias' to the paper by drawing it under a straightedge or the knife (if it is a small piece). Whenever the word 'bias' is used in this book it indicates this treatment. Next I cut any slots necessary for fixing the nose, eyelids, etc., which may be included in the diagram. Then I make any scores that may be needed and 'crease' them the necessary amount. Scores and slots should never be cut before biasing as this will make for uneven curvature and probable tearing. Sometimes I score the fixing tabs formed by extending the mask, so that they can fold sharply back behind the armature for gluing. On other occasions I 'spring' the tabs round behind the armature. This gives a better three-dimensional effect, but on sharp curves in stout paper care must be taken to 'bias' the tabs enough to prevent them tearing away from the armature. Experience soon teaches one how to cope with such technical problems and to find solutions as one goes along.

The heads of my high-relief constructions are rarely 'full-face'. More usually they range from almost full-face to profile. In many of these cases I use an extremely simple but effective way of interpreting, for example, the nose. This may be nothing more than a two-dimensional paper shape (sometimes with the nostril wing scored from behind and lifted out slightly). A typical example is the Pop Singer (page 33), from the Spirit of Youth figures, designed for a New Year's Eve Ball at the Albert Hall, where the nose is in complete profile and in fact integral with the face-mask itself from which it is cut, although the rest of the head is almost full-face. Perhaps this technique of showing profile and full-face simultaneously owes something to Picasso, though I have no recollection of being consciously influenced by him!

I often suggest eyes by attaching top and bottom lids (with or without eyelashes) to the mask, the eyeball and iris being simply a white paper unit with a circular hole, inserted behind the eyelid. At other times the iris can be a small paper cone. At still others, the top lid alone is enough to give expression to the eye.

Lips can be profiled as a pair from a single piece of paper and then curve-scored from behind at their junction. When this curved score is formed, the lips take up a crescent shape which follows the curve of the face mask and is fixed with impact adhesive.

Very heavy paper should always be used for large curved areas, such as coats and skirts, as the curvature then assumed has much more 'tension', is more rigid and a better base for applied detail. When constructing narrow conical and tubular shapes where there is practically no room for securing the paper to the armature, I overlap the edges of the cone or cylinder as much as possible *behind*, add a little impact glue between the overlaps and secure them with encircling rubber bands until the glue has set. A dowel threaded through the tube or cone while the glue is setting makes a useful pressure point against which the fingers can press the joint together. Any edges of the overlap showing from the front of the sculpture can be shaved off with the scalpel when the glue has set. Incidentally, these narrow tubular shapes should first be 'rolled' by working them around a dowel or metal tube with the fingers. This helps to stop the paper cracking under the stress of extreme bending. Whenever the expression 'rolling' is used in this book it applies to this process.

Nothing spoils the look of a sculpture more, in my opinion, than inaccurate scoring. Unscored folds look woolly and imprecise, and should be avoided. I make most of my straight scores with the straightedge and lightly held scalpel. There is another way of making straight scores which I use very occasionally. This is done by scoring on the *back* of the paper instead of the front, using a very blunt knife or suitable point, so that the paper is indented and crushed instead of cut. The paper can now be folded as with a cut score, and will be found to follow the lie of the indentation on the rear side. The advantages of this method is that the paper is not weakened along the line of the score, and also, as there is no actual cut, the paper does not 'open up' showing a double edge along the score line. The indented score is more difficult to make accurately however.

When constructing full-round paper sculptures my method of approach is very similar. I make an initial sketch from the most significant angle of view, developing and enlarging it as a master diagram. The diagram for the Elizabethan on page 65, for example, might almost as well have served for a full-round as for a high-relief figure. I would have followed the same procedure, starting with the head. However, instead of 'spreading' the mask as described earlier in this chapter, I would have formed it into a tapering cylinder by measuring across the upper and lower boundaries of the mask, multiplying by $3\frac{1}{7}$, bending round and securing behind with impact glue. ($3\frac{1}{7}$, you will remember from your geometry lessons at school, is the formula for translating the diameter of a circle into its circumference, and the extra bit (making $3\frac{1}{2}$) is for the overlapped join.) All the other fundamental parts of the sculpture would have been calculated in the same way. I would then have assembled them on an armature constructed of wood dowels, cardboard tubes, or any other convenient material to make a rigid support, using 'diaphragms' of cardboard where necessary to keep the paper structures in shape and to locate them correctly on the armature. Surface features would then have been added as to a high-relief sculpture. But on the full-round sculpture these would not be in false perspective, and several master diagrams of details, taken from different angles, would probably have been made in order to facilitate the completion of the sculpture. The chapter on the Cat will help to demonstrate the problems which arise when designing a full-round paper sculpture.

A study of the photographs throughout this book will show some of the variations which are possible in the design of paper sculpture figures.

Enlargement by the square-up process

Along the edges of each Cockatoo, Cat and Second King diagram will be found a set of equidistant marks. If these are ruled across from one side to the

The Dream of Gerontius—a magazine design

other a grid of squares will be formed, covering the entire diagram. I am not suggesting that you do this to the diagrams in the book but, when you trace them off, rule in these lines as well. In the case of the Cockatoo, for example, you will find you have 16 horizontal lines and 13 vertical ones. These should now be numbered, starting with No. 1 at the bottom left corner and numbering up to 16 on the left side of the grid, and to 13 along the bottom, the figure 1 being common to both sets of numbers.

Now draw a similar grid, with the same number of horizontal and vertical lines, on another piece of tracing paper, but this time space the lines 2 cm apart. This grid will, of course, be larger than the one you have traced from the book. Number the lines exactly as on the first grid. You can now enlarge the diagrams as traced from the book accurately on to the larger grid, using the

PANTONE
Präzisions-Reisszeug
de compas de précision
de compases de precisión
KernSwiss

Opposite *International City—constructed mainly in paper sculpture but also incorporating products manufactured by Letraset*

Above *Captain Cook and the Astronaut, for a beer poster*

intersection of the lines as reference points. The enlarged diagrams will be the same size as those in my original sculpture.

The same process applies to the diagrams for the Cat and Second King. In each case the line spacings of the grids should be enlarged to 2 cm. This will enlarge the diagrams in the book to the size of my originals.

When you want to enlarge one of your own original designs you draw a rectangle closely surrounding the design and divide it into a grid of squares. The size of the squares depends on the size of your drawing. If it is quite small, say 10 × 8 cm, the lines could be $\frac{1}{2}$ cm apart, making $\frac{1}{2}$ cm squares. The smaller and more numerous the squares, the greater the accuracy of the enlargement. But too many squares can be confusing, so you have to work out for yourself the number of squares to suit your design. Now you decide how large you wish the finished sculpture to be. Suppose it is to be 40 cm high. You then draw another rectangle the same proportion as your original one, i.e. measuring 40 × 32 cm. The corresponding lines on this rectangle will be 2 cm apart. After you have numbered both grids as described above you can start the enlargement.

Coloured paper sculpture

The 'purist' form of paper sculpture can be said to be that in white paper only, as this demands all the ingenuity of the designer in the creation of interesting and significant forms, without the help and added diversion of colour. When colour *is* required I always apply it after the sculpture is completed, by painting the surfaces, usually with poster or gouache colours and occasionally with acrylic paints. I never use transparent watercolours or inks because they are difficult to control and their 'wetness' will almost certainly cockle the paper.

I like all my colours to be completely 'flat' and uniform in tint as any variation would add yet another 'diversion' to the sculpture, impairing its unique paper quality. Poster colours (and the somewhat more subtle and expensive gouache

55

colours) are ideal for this as they have 'body' and are opaque, drying with a uniform flatness.

The colours should be prepared in small dishes or palettes (saucers will do) and water mixed in to give a consistency of cream—i.e. runny but not 'wet'. Enough should be mixed to cover the area required. If the colour is of the right consistency and applied quickly and evenly with a largish watercolour brush (preferably sable-haired) it should dry rapidly without affecting the paper. I prefer to use light tones as strong colours can add still more interference to the forms of the sculpture.

Although poster colours are very satisfactory in many ways they tend to fade with time and are not particularly 'brilliant'. Recently I designed a large full-round Peacock for an exposition in Nigeria. Intense glowing colour was wanted for this and I found that acrylics gave the best effect. These are bound in a transparent water-emulsion of acrylic polymer resin and can be mixed with various mediums, including one that gives a glossy surface, greatly enhancing the brilliance of the colour. Acrylics are somewhat less simple to use than poster colours however and I would advise learning a little about them before use. A useful little book on the subject is *Painting with Acrylic Colours* by Alwyn Crawshaw (Rowney). Poster and acrylic colours can be bought at art material suppliers.

I have been asked why I never use coloured papers. There are several reasons for this. One is that coloured papers are not made in the quality best suited for paper sculpture. Another is that the colours available are not wide enough in range— and if they were I should have to keep a large stock of rarely-used colours on hand to be sure that I had exactly the ones I needed when required. And a third reason is that it is impossible to visualise the range and distribution of the colours I will need before the sculpture is completed. With a little experience, painting is so easy and flexible that there is little point in trying to achieve colour by any other means.

Portrait Sculpture

This is a very specialised branch of paper sculpture and one which depends, for a start, entirely on the artist's talent for likeness and caricature.

When asked by the publisher to write a section on portraiture a problem presented itself at the outset—that of not wishing to step on the toes and sensitivities of recently 'taken' subjects. I know I should not personally appreciate being dismantled, muscle by muscle, and dewlap by dewlap, for the purpose of demonstrating technique in a book on paper sculpture. And I am sure you would not either.

So I have gone back into the pages of history—right back to the Second World War in fact, when, though quite young and learning, I produced a whole series of full-round sculpture portraits of famous wartime characters. The most famous of these, Stalin, Roosevelt, Chamberlain, Beaverbrook, etc., had already been through the mill of caricature at the hands of masters like David Low and Vicky, who had thus done all the preliminary analysis of salient features. As a result my portraits of these figures contain a greater element of caricature than those, such as 'Bomber' Harris, for whom I had to rely on snapshotted press photographs. I have included with each paper sculpture portrait a press photograph taken at about the time the sculpture was made so that you can see for yourself how the various facial shapes were developed.

I set about making these portraits exactly as described in Methods of Working. First surrounding myself with as many press photographs and caricatures as I could find, I developed a highly finished pencil drawing, carefully shaded to indicate form and intended to resemble, as closely as possible, the projected sculpture. From this I could plan the basic foundation head shape and many of the facial units. Sometimes, particularly when I had enough suitable references, I made a profile drawing as well, but on no occasion did I meet the subject personally, nor was I able to specify what photographs I wanted.

One of the first I attempted was the portrait of Joseph Stalin, made during the early years of the war before the invasion of Russia. Stalin was something of an enigma at that time and I tried to bring out his inscrutability in the sculpture. The significant features of Stalin's face were the prominent eyebrows, thick black hair and moustache, plus the downturned nose, heavy lower lip, jutting chin and full neck. You will see that the eyes are just suggested by the top lids only, that the jowl behind the cheek is a simple flat shape running from the corner of the eye to the chin and the high cheekbone is suggested by the angled ellipse from the nose to the cheek.

Another early sculpture was the one of Franklin D. Roosevelt, President of the United States during the war. He was fixed in the mind of the public as a strong, sunny, laughing figure with an enormous chin and pince-nez. In common with several of the portraits in this series it was made in full-round without glue, interlocking tabs of various kinds being used to hold the sculpture together. In the Roosevelt sculpture you will see the importance of the slightly tipped-back head angle, the strong, optimistic chin and the angles of the mouth areas. In life the lips were not pronounced, and are not indicated at all in the sculpture. The teeth are an important part of the smile; also the prominent screwed-up eyes. The pince-nez, surprisingly, are very important. On the sculpture they were indicated by a simple silhouette of cellophane, with a wisp of white paint lightly airbrushed across to suggest glint.

Neville Chamberlain was another sculpture made on the interlocking principle. Here the chin is pronounced but not aggressive. The lower lip is

Joseph Stalin

Neville Chamberlain

Franklin D. Roosevelt

'Bomber' Harris

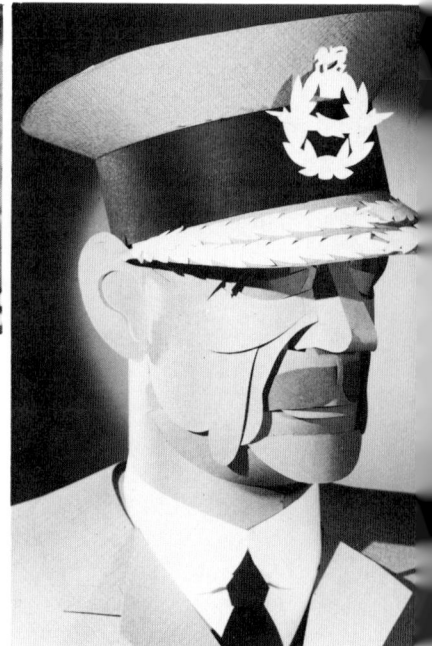

Lord Beaverbrook

Sir Samuel Hoare

very prominent (indicated by a flat shape in an almost horizontal plane). The aquiline nose, heavy moustache and eyebrows are significant, and the way they are interpreted can be clearly seen in the photograph of the sculpture.

'Bomber' Harris's face was also moustached, and with a strong chin and compressed lower lip. The interpretation of these characteristics is similar to that of Neville Chamberlain, but whereas Mr Chamberlain's diplomatic tranquillity is suggested by the flowing nature of the 'character' lines, and the lines of the hair, 'Bomber' Harris's grim determination is evidenced by the narrowed, lined eyes and the more broken lines of the face.

Lord Beaverbrook became Aircraft Production Minister in 1940. As a newspaper proprietor he often featured in cartoons by David Low and others. Important features of his face were the beetling eyebrows, wide full mouth and watchful eyes. In the sculpture great emphasis is placed on these elements and on the full cheek line.

Sir Samuel Hoare had a lean, smiling face, with long straight nose, beetling eyebrows, strong chin and narrowed eyes. This sculpture shows clearly the character lines on a taut but expressive face. The way the cheekbone is suggested and the smile-lines in mid-cheek show how varied can be the methods used in paper sculpture interpretation.

Materials

I do not want to be dogmatic about the array of tools and materials necessary to create paper sculpture. Obviously you will need a pair of scissors and a sharp knife, plus a surface to cut on. Also a pencil, adhesive, an eraser and suitable paper are essential. Armed with these basic materials and sufficient inspiration, interesting effects can obviously be produced.

Artists work in different ways and you will be as capable as I was to discover the tools best suited to your purpose. However, as this is a book based entirely on my own experience, it will be logical if I list all the tools I use personally. You don't have to buy them all at once, of course.

Blade holder with detachable blades   Until a few years ago I used a surgeon's scalpel with clip-on No. 11 blades, but since then an assortment of similar devices for use outside the operating theatre has come on the market and can be bought at most art material suppliers. These are available with a variety of blade shapes, including the No. 11 (narrow and pointed). I have since found that a variation (No. 10A) is better as it is slightly less narrow and therefore less likely to snap under pressure. A snapped blade can be dangerous, as it tends to fly up in your face, so take care.

Dry carborundum stone   for sharpening slightly dulled blades. These soon lose their fine cutting point and can be resharpened with a few strokes on the carborundum stone. The stone can be quite small—about 8×2 cm (3×1 in) wide. They can be bought at hardware stores and ironmongers.

Sheet of glass   for a cutting surface. This should be about $\frac{1}{2}$ cm ($\frac{1}{4}$ in) thick, with polished edges. The plate-glass shelves used in bathrooms are suitable, say about 60×15 cm (24×6 in). I find glass is much the best substance for cutting on.

Heavy metal straightedge   at least 50 cm (20 in) long, for guiding the knife on straight lines. Also for 'biasing' (see page 52). From a good hardware shop or art material suppliers.

Scissors   Good quality ones of medium size. From hardware stores.

Metal shears   Useful when cutting sheet aluminium for armatures. Also for cutting microply. The sort with scissor-type handles are best. From hardware stores.

Pinking shears   Invaluable for decorative zigzag edge effects. From the haberdashery section of a department store.

Stapler   The small hand-held type is suitable. A staple-gun can also be very useful when working on large-scale sculptures. From stationery suppliers.

Ruler or steel tape measure   divided in centimetres. From hardware stores and stationers.

Draughtsman's pencil compasses   with an extending arm for striking large circles. From art material shops.

Pair of dividers   From art material shops.

Ordinary table knife   with a slightly curved (blunt) cutting edge for 'biasing' paper (see page 52). Also for rubbing down diagrams (see page 49). From the kitchen drawer.

Several rods, tubes or dowels   of various thicknesses from $\frac{1}{2}$ to 3 cm ($\frac{1}{5}$ to 1 in) diameter and about 30 cm (12 in) long. These are useful for 'rolling' (see page 53). From builders merchants, DIY shops and hardware stores.

Impact adhesives in collapsible tubes   I use Bostik Clear and Uhu. There is nothing to choose between them for efficiency, but Uhu has a fine nozzle which controls the adhesive more effectively. From hardware stores.

Supply of balsa wood   about $\frac{1}{2}$ cm ($\frac{1}{4}$ in) thick. From DIY and model-making shops.

Sheets of microply   about $1\frac{1}{2}$ mm ($\frac{1}{16}$ in) thick or less. Microply is a very thin plywood, made of three layers. DIY shops and model-making shops should be able to supply it.

Tweezers   From a pharmaceutical store.

Small bench vice   From a hardware store.

Drill with bits   From a hardware store or DIY shop.

Small tenon saw   From a hardware store.

Square-section awl   for boring screw holes in wood. From a hardware store.

Screwdriver   From a hardware store or DIY shop.

Pliers   From a hardware store.

Punch for cutting circular holes   I use a scissor-type leather punch with a range of cutters. From a haberdashery store.

Elastic bands and bulldog clips   From a stationers.

Pencils, watercolour brushes and an eraser   From an art materials shop.

A supply of poster, gouache or acrylic colours   From an art materials shop.

Electric jig-saw   From a hardware store or DIY shop.

Large wastepaper basket   Probably already in your home.

Construction and other paper

The paper used in the construction of paper sculpture must be very flexible—able to withstand bending to quite small radii without cracking. It should also have a hard white surface. For these reasons paper made of wood fibre, e.g. cartridge paper, is not really suitable.

The most suitable paper ever made for paper sculpture was Whatman which was made largely of linen rags, the fibres of which were woven by a special process invented by the founder of the company in the eighteenth century. Like so many invaluable hand-made products, Whatman paper went out of production in the 1960s.

Generally speaking, the most suitable papers available today are the so-called watercolour papers. Of these I have listed the following makes—all of which come in sheets approximately 50×75 cm (20×30 in) in size.

Fabriano 160 gm (lightweight)
Fabriano 200 gm (medium)
Fabriano 300 gm (heavy)
Saunders 72 lb (very light)
Saunders 90 lb (lightweight)
Saunders 140 lb (medium)
Saunders 200 lb (heavy)
Rockingford 150 gm (lighweight)
Rockingford 190 gm (medium)
Rockingford 300 gm (heavy)

I offer these makes because they are probably most readily available at art material shops. Other makes are equally suitable. The important thing is that they contain cotton, or preferably linen, fibres. You should buy the most expensive paper you can afford.

It is advisable to have two or three weights of paper on hand—the lightest weights for small, intricate parts and the heavier ones for larger, simpler areas. As a general rule one should use the heaviest paper that one can. Different makes of paper should not be used on the same sculpture as the colour and surface texture varies considerably between manufacturers' products.

Most watercolour papers come in three surfaces: Hot Pressed (very smooth), Not Pressed (slight texture) and Rough (coarse texture). I prefer the Not Pressed surfaces myself as the texture avoids unwanted sheen and the surface takes colour better.

Other papers which will be required in the creation of paper sculpture are detail and tracing paper. Detail paper, which can be bought in rolls and pads of various sizes, is semi-translucent and is useful when developing a design from rough form to detailed plan. When a piece of detail paper is placed over the rough conception of a design, the shapes can be seen sufficiently well to act as a guide for further development. Detail paper varies considerably in translucency, some types being too opaque to be of much use for the purpose just described. Recommended types are: GAF 101A and Causer & Co's No 98. Incidentally, ordinary grease-proof cooking paper is quite good!

Tracing paper, also obtainable in rolls and pads, is much more transparent than detail paper and is useful for tracing off finished designs and shapes where clarity is essential. You should use tracing paper, for example, when transferring and scaling up the diagrams in this book. Most types of tracing paper are acceptable, though it is best to avoid the oiled variety.

Sherlock Holmes in corrugated packing paper, for a paper manufacturer

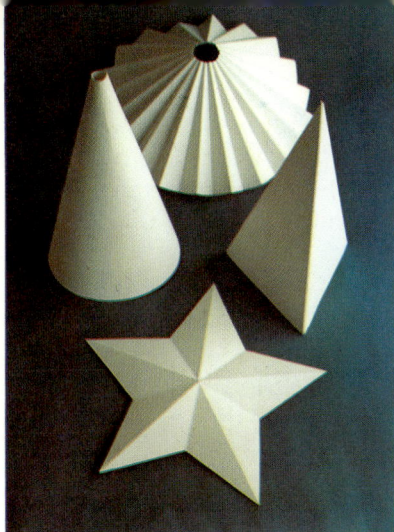

Fundamental Forms

When a piece of paper is folded or bent it ceases to be a two-dimensional object and becomes the beginning of a paper sculpture, for folding and bending are the only ways in which paper can be treated sculpturally. From these fundamentals arise seven basic forms: cones; cylinders; box forms; accordion pleats; concave and convex pleats; straight, curved and compound scores.

Cones and cylinders are the foundation shapes of much full-round paper sculpture. Their natural rigidity forms an excellent base upon which to build up the rest of the structure and it is most important to establish this rigidity at an early stage.

Cylinders and tubes are made from rectangular pieces of paper, rolled round and cemented at the opposing edges. Large-diameter cylinders do not have the inherent rigidity of cones, though heavy-gauge paper helps to overcome this to a great extent. Narrow cylinders and tubes are much more naturally rigid.

Cones are made from parts of a circle, small sectors making slender cones, near-complete circles making wide, flat ones.

Box forms are used in pyramidal, cubic and other flat-sided three-dimensional shapes. They can be useful as structural supports, for plinths and so on.

Accordion pleats must be designed very accurately as unless they are carefully spaced they give a coarse effect. They should always be mounted over a foundation to which each separate pleat is cemented, to avoid a haphazard look. Accordion pleats have no inherent rigidity, but when attached to their underlying foundation paper this defect is reversed and the composite structure can have great stability.

Concave and convex pleats merit the same warnings as accordion pleats. These pleats are formed from scores all made on the same side of the paper, i.e. on the surface side in the case of concave pleats, not alternately on front and back as in accordion pleats. Before scoring, the paper is given a cylindrical 'bias' by pulling it under a straight-edge held firmly against the working table or glass cutting surface.

Curved scores always seem to puzzle people who have never attempted paper sculpture but there is no mystery about them. The paper is simply scored along a curved line instead of a straight one. When bent along the score the paper is automatically distorted three-dimensionally. When curved scores are made alternately on the surface and underside of the paper, the distortions tend to cancel out and the overall area of the paper

63

remains substantially in a flat plane; but a single curved score can result in marked changes of plane and curvature. Certain types of curved score, e.g. S-shaped scores, cause the paper to warp in various surprising ways.

Compound scores work on the same mechanical principles as curved scores, resulting in a pattern of differing surface angles created at the expense of an overall shrinkage of the paper area.

As both curved and compound scores are seldom met with in the ordinary, everyday handling of paper objects, their imaginative use in paper sculpture can impart a plastic quality creating unfamiliar and intriguing effects.

Spreading

The head of the Elizabethan shown opposite illustrates the method of 'spreading' parts of the master drawing to allow for their interpretation in three dimensions (see page 49). Fig. 1 is the master drawing; Fig. 2 is the armature of the head; Fig. 3 is the mask of the face.

The mask is traced off the master drawing by the following method: a centre line XY is drawn on the master drawing and also on a piece of tracing paper. The paper is then laid over the drawing with the lines in register. The front of the mask up to approximately points P is then traced off the master drawing, including any slots for nose, lip and eye tabs, etc. The sides of the mask are then 'spread' by moving the tracing, first to the left of the centre line and finishing the *right* side of the mask, and then to the right of the centre line and finishing the *left* side of the mask. Lines AB and A1B1 show the original and 'spread' positions of the sides of the mask. The mounting tabs C and D are then formed for attaching the mask to the armature as shown in Fig. 4.

The only other part of this design which needs to be 'spread' is the hat unit (Fig. 6). It will be seen that the 'spread' lines A1B1 follow the taper of the rest of the unit. This is because the hat is conical and requires less 'spreading' at the narrow end. Fig. 4A shows the hat unit in position.

The finished figure of the Elizabethan appears on p. 6 of this book.

The Whale in corrugated packing paper, for a paper manufacturer

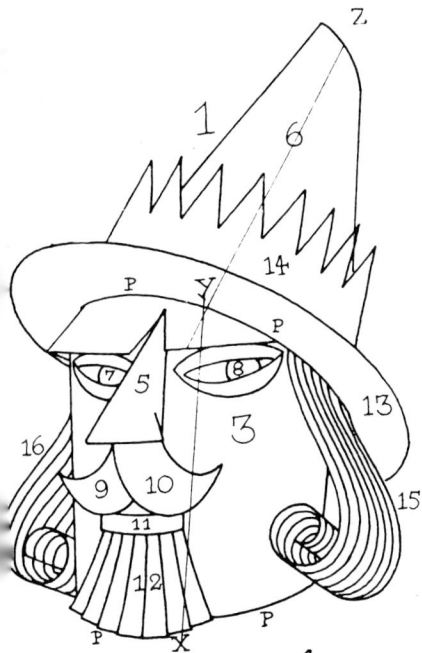

1

6

14

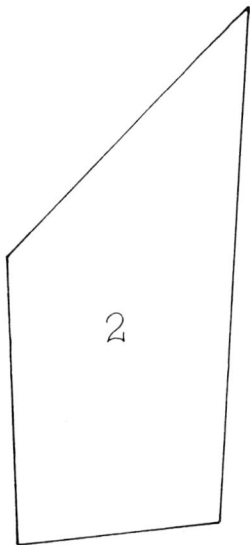

2

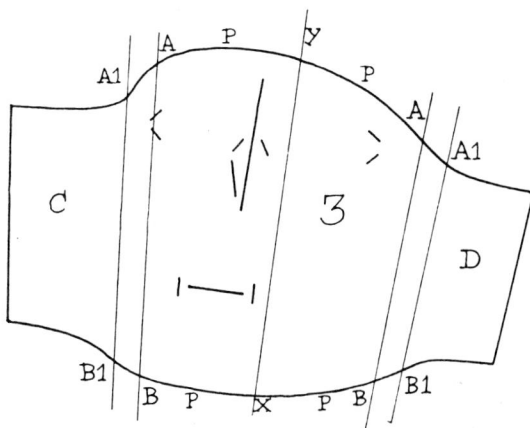

A1   A   P   Y   P   A
A1   A   A1
C   3   D
B1   B1
B   P   X   P   B

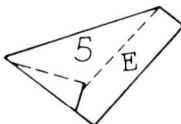

7

8

5   E

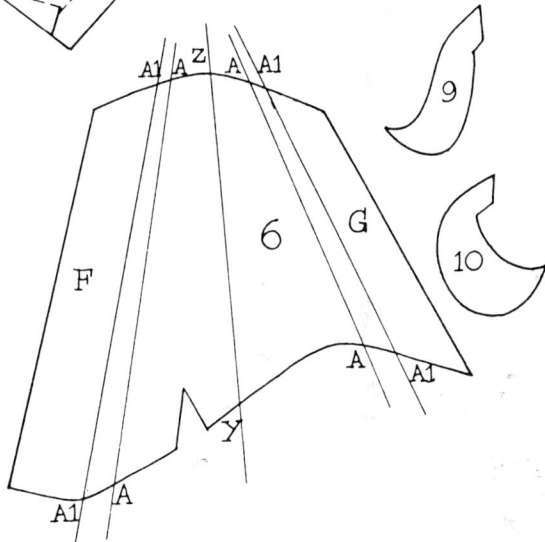

A1 Z A A1
F   6   G
A   A1
A1   A
Y

9

10

4

4A

11

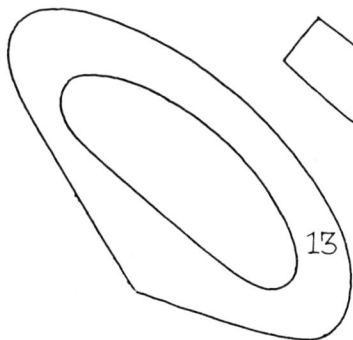

12

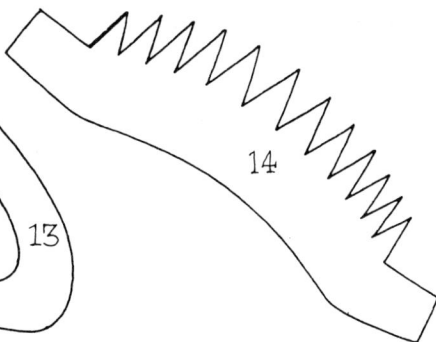

13

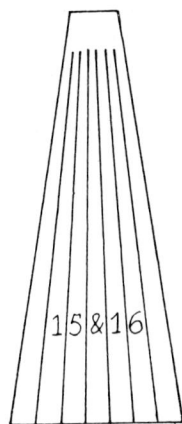

14

15 & 16

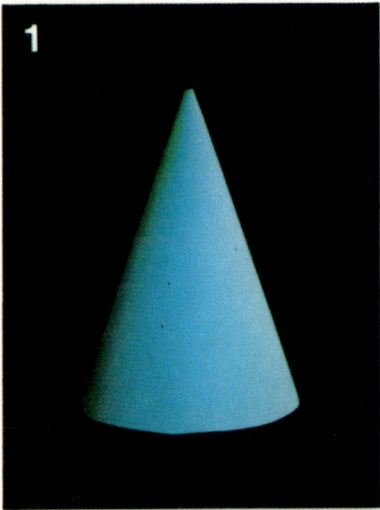

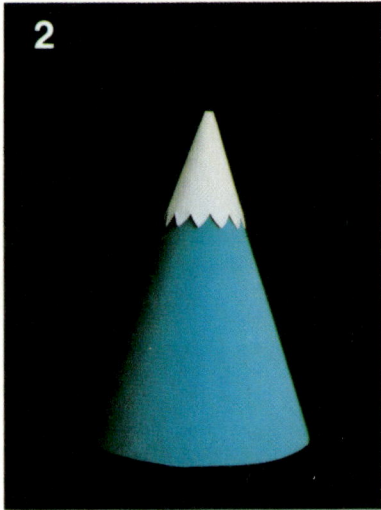

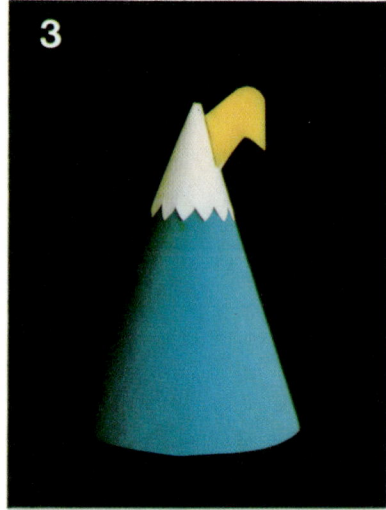

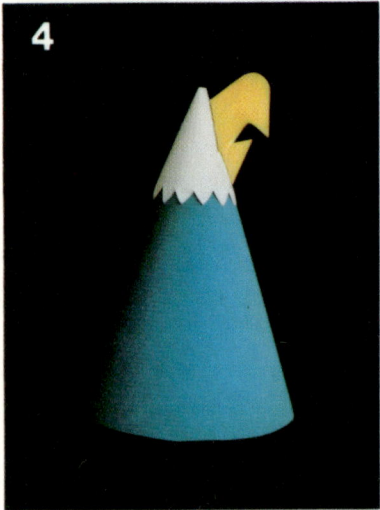

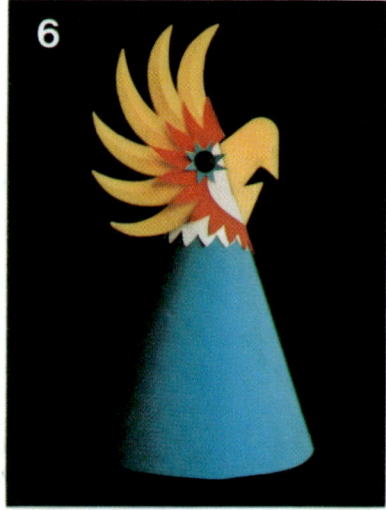

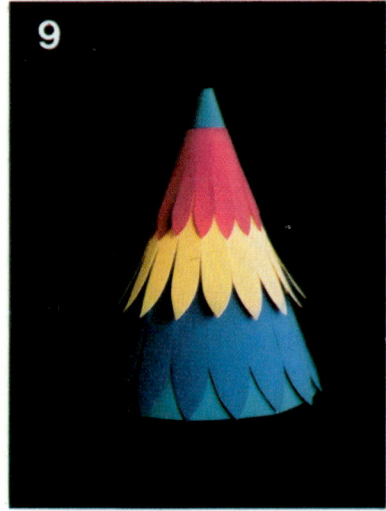

The Cockatoo

I have designed this easy-to-construct full-round paper sculpture as an exercise for the beginner, at the same time endeavouring to include as many of the basic principles, e.g. accurate cutting, stable basic structure without armature, curved scoring, point and tab gluing, as I can. I have also used colour as an additional exercise.

Two of the units—units 1 and 10—are too large to reproduce entire in this book without excessive reduction in scale of all the other units. As they are both symmetrical I have overcome this problem by reproducing only half of each of them. The other halves are identical mirror-images of the halves shown, the cross-hatched lines X-X being the centre lines of the two units. (The ragged edges simply indicate that the units are incomplete in the diagram.)

The diagrams should now be transferred to tracing paper and enlarged to the correct size by the square-up process (see page 53).

All the units should be cut out and painted before the Cockatoo is put together. This is to simplify the work of construction for the beginner. When you paint an original sculpture, however, or if you would like to vary my colour scheme on this one, it is better to paint the sculpture *after* it is made, so that you can judge the relationship between the colours more accurately. The poster colours used in the original sculpture are:

Body Cone (1) Rowney's Blue Lake
Beaks (3 and 4) Crest (5) Feathers (9) and Feathers (11) Rowney's Primrose Yellow
Ruff (6) Rowney's Permanent Orange
Eye Fringe (7) Rowney's Blue Lake
Eye (8) Black
Lower Feathers (10) Rowney's Cobalt Blue
Upper Feathers (12) Rowney's Brilliant Rose
Head Cone (2) White

The Body Cone (1) can now be made up. It is first 'biased' by pulling it between the straightedge and the working surface, so that it can be curved into a conical shape without risk of cracking the paper (see page 52). The edges are now overlapped by about 1 cm ($\frac{1}{3}$ in) and glued (Fig. 1). The Head Cone (2) is formed similarly (Fig. 2).

The Upper Beak (3) is now made up by scoring along a-a, b-b, c-c, and c-d, all on the upper, or front, side of the paper, and folding back along the scores. The tab G is now glued to the back of the opposing side at the top of the beak. When this has set sufficiently (after about one minute) the tabs E and F are overlapped and glued, forming a triangle at the back of the beak where it will be attached to the head. The base of the triangle should measure about 2 cm ($\frac{3}{4}$ in). Now the Upper Beak can be glued to the Head Cone on the side opposite to the join, in the position shown (Fig. 3). Before gluing, the triangular area at the back of the beak (which is the point of contact with the head) should be given a concave bias by rolling over a $\frac{1}{2}$ cm ($\frac{1}{5}$ in) dowel with your finger inside the beak. This will enable it to fit snugly to the Head Cone.

The Lower Beak (4) is now made up by scoring along a-a, b-a, c-a (front surface of the paper) and folding back. Score a-a forms the centre ridge of the beak. The tabs D and E are overlapped and glued, forming an inverted triangle measuring just under 2 cm ($\frac{3}{4}$ in) along the upper edge. This triangle is the point of attachment to the head, and should be given a concave bias as described above. The Lower Beak is now attached in the position shown (Fig. 4). (The top of the Lower Beak lies just inside the lower edge of the Upper Beak.)

The Crest (5) is double-sided, requiring two parts, one as shown in the diagram and the other its mirror-image. For complete accuracy this should be done by cutting both parts simultaneously. Cut a piece of paper just over double the width of the Crest and fold it down the centre. Trace the Crest down on to one of the folds and cut through both leaves of the folded paper simultaneously. With a sharp scalpel this is quite easy. Both sides of the Crest will now be identical. Now score the curved lines a-a (front surface) and b-b (rear surface) on one of the Crest pieces. Gently crease along the scores but do not fold them too deeply. Now crease along the rear-side scores b-b similarly.

The half-Crest will now lie flat on the cutting surface but will have a three-dimensional embossed effect. Do the same to the other part of the Crest, but make the scores from the opposite sides, so that you finish with two mirror-image units. Now place touches of impact adhesive such as Uhu on the inside of the points of one of the Crest pieces and also at C. Then gently stick the two pieces together by these glued points. After a moment or two the glue will hold and you will have the completed three-dimensional Crest.

Now the Crest assembly can be fixed to the head. This is simply slipped over the Head Cone as shown in Fig. 5. The lower edges of the Crest straddle the lower part of the Head Cone, while the top (which was previously glued together at c) just hooks over the top of the Head Cone, to which a touch of glue has been applied. The Crest assembly is also glued to the Head Cone at points d and d (Fig. 5).

The Ruff (6) has a single cut e-e and can now be added to the head, with the cut-through parts at the top. These are glued as closely as possible to the top front of the Crest, on each side, and also at points F and F (Fig. 6).

Now the Eye Fringe (7) and the Eye (8) are assembled. The roots of the Eye Fringe are scored along the dotted lines (rear side) and the fringes folded forwards slightly. The Eye (8) has a single cut from the outer edge to the centre point. By rolling this into a conical shape, using the pointed end of a propelling pencil or the end of a watercolour brush as 'former', the two edges of the cut can be overlapped slightly and glued. The Eye now assumes a conical shape and can be glued to the centre of the Eye Fringe, using touches of glue around the base of the cone. The Eye with Eye Fringe can now be glued to the Ruff at the position shown (Fig. 6).

The small Unit 9 can next be glued behind the Ruff as shown in Fig. 10. This conceals the straight edge of the Crest. Duplicates of the Eye assembly and Unit 9 should be attached on the opposite side of the head. The Lower Tier of Feathers (10) can next be attached to the lower part of 1 as shown (Fig. 7) by gluing along its top edge only. The overlap of the ends of 10 should lie over the overlap of 1.

Feather units 11 and 12 are attached in the same way as 10. The feather-points of 11 should lie about 5 cm (2 in) up from the base of the Body Cone and should line up with the cuts between its feathers (Fig. 8). The points of 12 should lie about $11\frac{1}{2}$ cm ($4\frac{1}{2}$ in) up from the base of the Body Cone, i.e. about 5 cm (2 in) above those of 11 and again the points of 12 should lie over the cuts of 11 (Fig. 9). The overlaps of both these units should lie over those of 10.

Now the head assembly is placed on top of the Body Cone and the Cockatoo is complete (Fig. 10).

COCKATOO UNITS

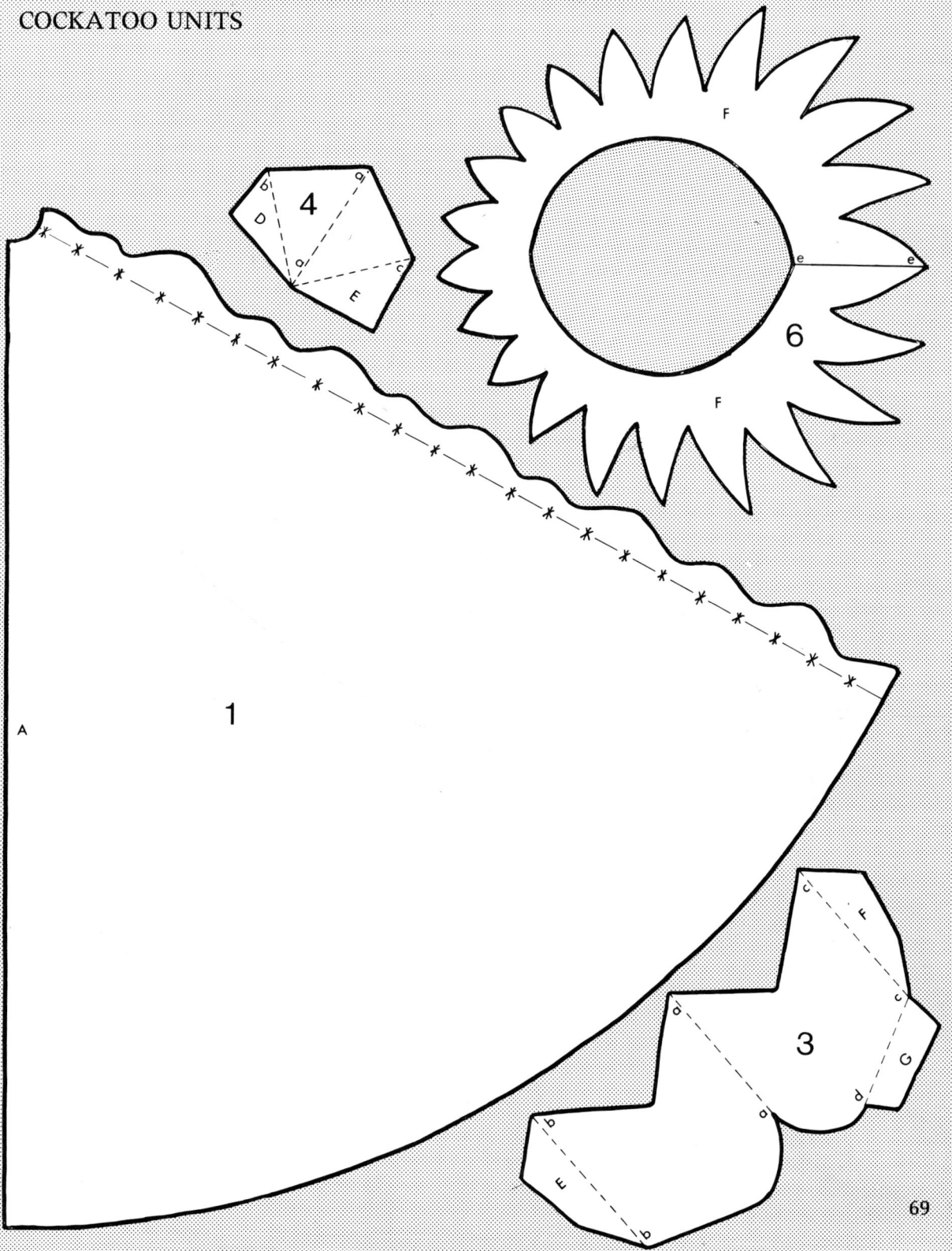

4

b

D

a

c

o

E

F

e

e

6

F

1

A

3

c

F

a

c

G

d

b

E

b

o

d

COCKATOO UNITS

5

9

2

8

7

10

COCKATOO UNITS

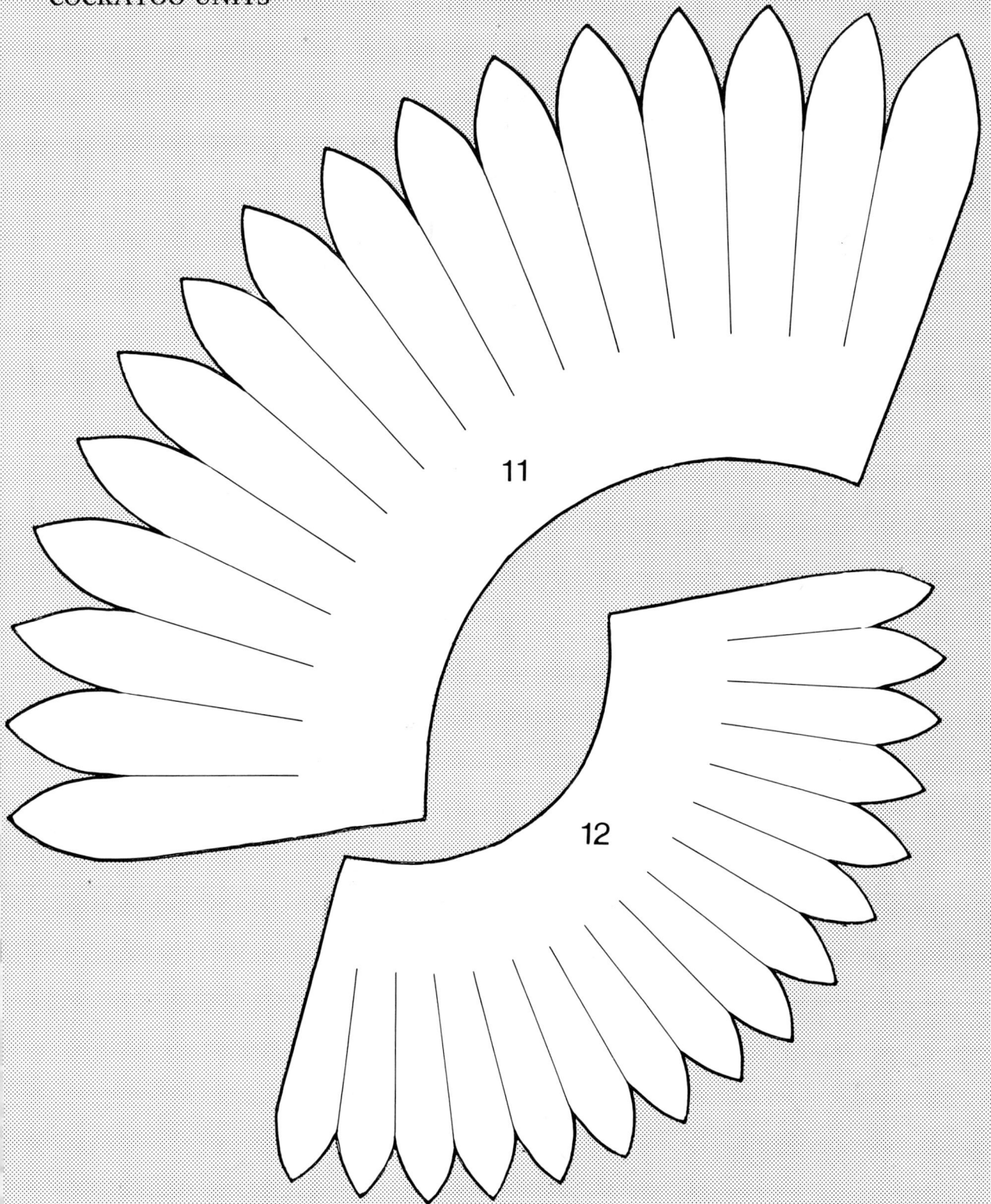

11

12

The Cat

When I first designed this full-round sculpture I worked to an overall height of 20 cm (8 in). To get all the working diagrams into this book it has been necessary for me to reduce them in size. The diagrams should therefore first be traced on to tracing paper and then enlarged to full size (preferably on detail paper) and drawn in pencil by the square-up process (see page 53). Several of the units are symmetrical in shape so, to ensure that they are reproduced as large as possible in the comparatively small format of this book, I have taken the largest of these units, numbers 1, 5, 6 and 7, and cut them in half, reproducing only one side. In each case the missing side is easily replaced by duplicating it as a mirror-image (including letter-code marks) using the thin black cross-hatched line as a centre line (the ragged end of these diagrams is simply an indication that they have been cut away). Unit 8 is an example of a similar unit which is small enough to reproduce entire.

When completed the enlarged diagrams can be turned over and rubbed down on to the construction paper (page 49) and then carefully cut out (page 49). The surfaces of the units bearing the rubbed-down pencil marks will, of course, be on the 'wrong' side. By the simple process of turning the units over as you use them you will have nice clean surfaces, the right way round and free of pencil marks.

Now start the construction with Unit 1 which is the foundation cone of the sculpture. Bend this round in a cone shape, curling or 'rolling' the front edges A-A inwards and gluing them together at the points X (Fig. 1). It is advisable to use a dowel or tube 2 cm ($\frac{3}{4}$ in) in diameter to act as a shaper when curling these front edges as this helps to avoid cracking of the paper.

The legs (2) and (3) are now 'rolled' into cylinders using the dowel (see page 53) and glued

all along their overlapping edges at Y. Unit 4 is made up in the same way. Glue the two legs to this (Fig. 2). Make sure that the joined areas of the leg units are not visible from the front or sides.

Now mount this triple tube assembly on the front of Unit 1 (Fig. 3), gluing along the points of contact. The narrower tube of Unit 4 should fit neatly into the indentation of Unit 1, forming a rigid foundation for the sculpture. The 'feet' ends of the leg units should of course line up with the bottom of Unit 1.

The fringe (5) is added next. Fold the tabs A right back at the score lines. Wrap Unit 5 round the back of Unit 1 at the base, gluing the folded tabs each side of and close to the leg units (Fig. 4). The points of the fringe should be bent outwards by shaping them between finger and thumb. The fringe (6) is now bent round in a cone shape and the overlapping edges A glued together. Curve out the points of the fringe between finger and thumb and slide the unit over the Unit 1 leg assembly, gluing at points Y (Fig. 4). The top edge of Unit 6 should line up with the top of Unit 1 (Fig. 5).

Unit 7 is made up similarly and glued in place at points Z (Fig. 5) over Unit 6, the top edge also lining up with that of Unit 1 (Fig. 6).

Head Unit 8, after the slots L and J have been cut, is now made up in the same way as Units 6 and 7. The eight tabs on the top edge are bent inwards along the score lines (Fig. 7). Now take top Unit 9, after cutting slots K and H, and impart to it a convex curved shape by turning over and 'biasing' it between a straight edge and the glass cutting surface (page 52), so that it will fit snugly over the top of Unit 8. Before gluing, the 'nose' area B of Unit 9 must be shaped with a 1 cm ($\frac{1}{3}$ in) dowel to curve downwards at each side (Fig. 8).

Unit 9 is now placed over the top of Unit 8 and carefully lined up so that the 'nose' area is at the front (exactly opposite to the glued joint at the

back of Unit 8). The two units, held together in the cup of the left hand, are turned upside-down and the two tabs at the front and back of Unit 8 are glued to the underside of Unit 9. The top edge of Unit 8 should now be adjusted so that it lies close to the inner edges of the fringe serrations all the way round Unit 9 (Fig. 9). The six tabs that are remaining can now be glued to the underside of Unit 9.

Units 10, 13 and 14 give a furry appearance to the sides of the cat's face. Before fixing Unit 10, the muzzle Unit 11 is made up. This is a small, somewhat complicated unit which should be set up with care as it is very important for the 'look' of the cat. After you have cut out Unit 11 the tabs C are scored from the front. The two slots D are cut through and the centre line of the muzzle is scored from behind. The whole unit is then 'rolled' over a 1 cm ($\frac{1}{3}$ in) dowel and the two sides of the muzzle are bent forward at the scored centre line. The muzzle should then look like Fig. 10. The two tabs E are now curved over towards each other and glued at the point of overlap (Fig. 11).

Unit 11 is now fitted to Unit 10 by pushing the tabs C through the corresponding slots on Unit 10, then folding them behind and gluing (Fig. 12).

Unit 10 is next glued to the front area of the head Unit 8 with its lower straight line lying over the tops of the four central fringe serrations. The left and right extremities of Unit 10 should not be stuck closely to the head Unit 8 but stand away a couple of centimetres at each side. Thus Unit 10 should be glued only at the centre at points about 4 cm ($1\frac{1}{2}$ in) in from each extremity (Fig. 13).

The nose Unit 12 is glued in position (Fig. 13). The chin Unit 27 is also added at this stage, after scoring the tabs F. The unit should be 'rolled' to a convex curve with a dowel and the tabs bent behind. Glue is then put on the tabs and the unit placed in position behind and under the muzzle. (In awkward places like this the blade of the kitchen knife can be used to press the tabs while the glue is setting.)

Next the cheek fringe Units 13 and 14 are fitted each side of the muzzle and glued in place by their previously folded-back tabs G (Fig. 13). Now the eye-back Units 15 and 16 are mounted on small pieces of balsa wood, about 2 mm ($\frac{1}{12}$ in) thick, which in turn are glued to the cheek fringes. Visual positioning is extremely important here and the photograph of the finished sculpture should be studied carefully during construction.

The eye-front Units 17 and 18 are now prepared, the 'pupils' being cut out and the whole eye-front given a convex curvature by rolling over a dowel. They are then fixed over the eye-back units with a touch of glue at their two side extremities, so that the centre part of the eye-front, bearing the pupil, is located about 3 mm ($\frac{1}{10}$ in) in front of the eye-back (Fig. 14).

The top eyelids are now added (Units 19 and 20), first 'rolling' them into a curve with a dowel so that they lie snugly over the top of the eye and then gluing them in position. The same process is applied to the lower eyelids 21 and 22 (Fig. 14).

The left and right eyebrows, 23 and 24, are now glued just behind top back of the eyes (Fig. 14).

The left and right whiskers, 25 and 26, can now be fixed by pushing them through the slots D in the muzzle and gluing behind (Fig. 15).

The ears, 28 and 29, are concave-curved by rolling and fitted into slots HJ and KL by the corresponding tabs, fixing with a touch of glue (Fig. 15).

The tail is glued under the back edge of Unit 1 by the six tabs and looped up behind the body. Another spot of glue attaches the tail to the back of Unit 7 (Figure 16).

The feet (31) are glued under the base of the legs, after giving each individual toe a convex form by rolling, using a 1 cm ($\frac{1}{3}$ in) dowel (Fig. 16).

The head can now be fixed to the body. A few spots of glue are placed near the top side of Unit 7 and the head slid over, being adjusted visually for angle, before the glue sets (Fig. 17). The finished Cat can now be glued to a suitable baseboard.

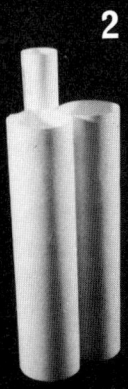

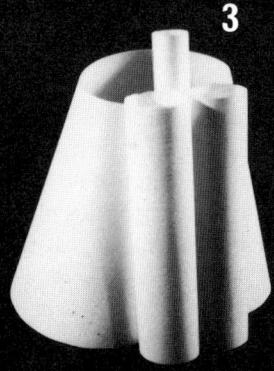

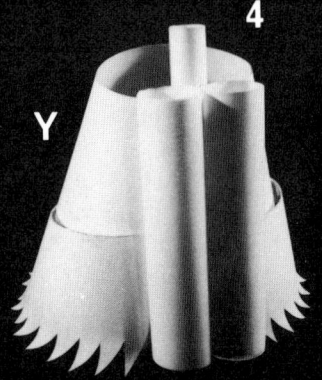

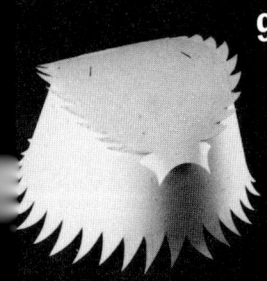

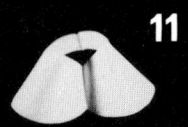

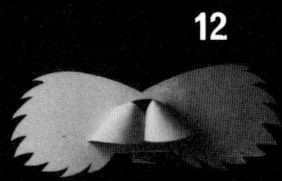

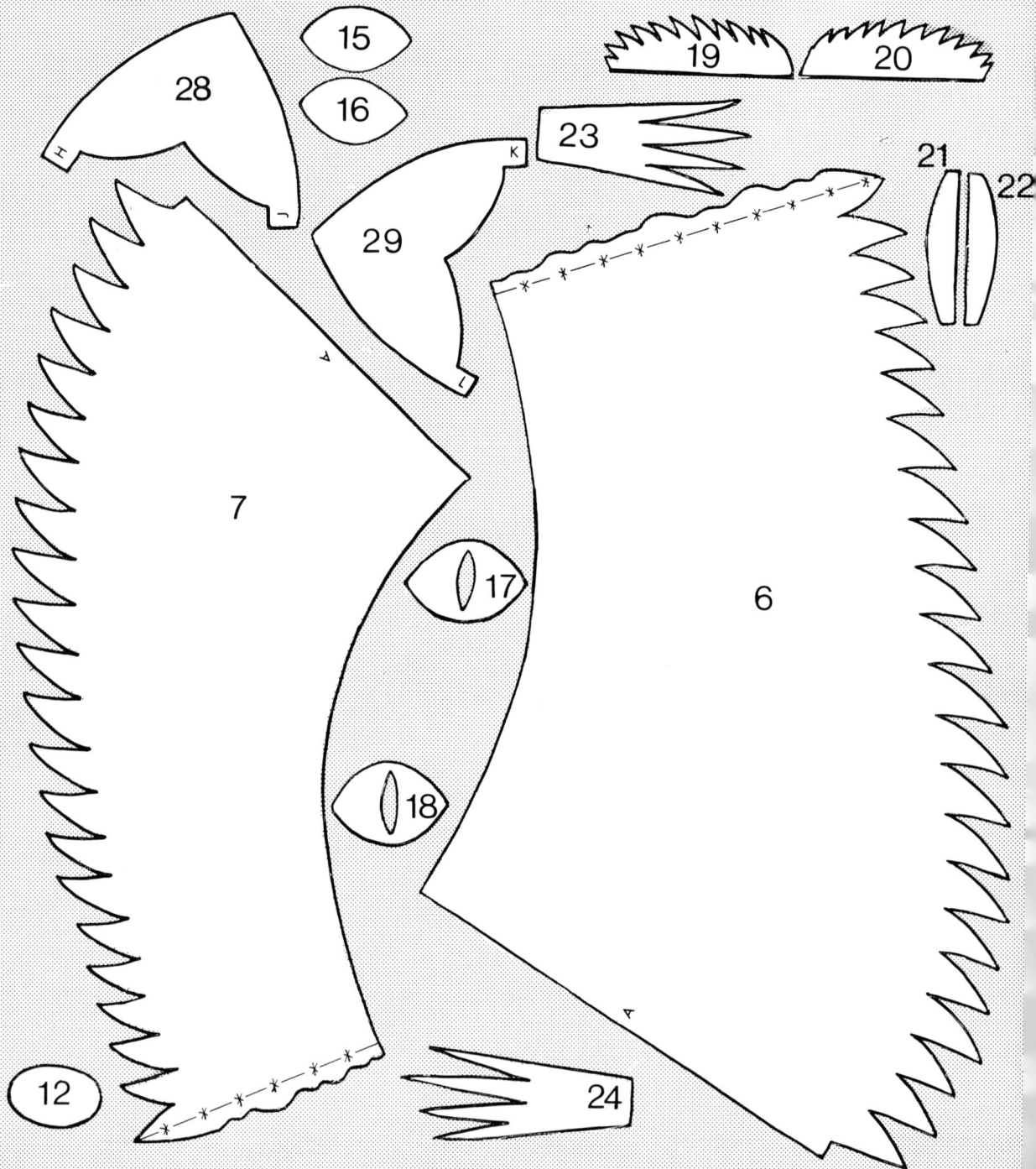

CAT UNITS

28

15

16

19

20

23

21

22

29

H

J

K

L

7

17

6

18

12

24

CAT UNITS

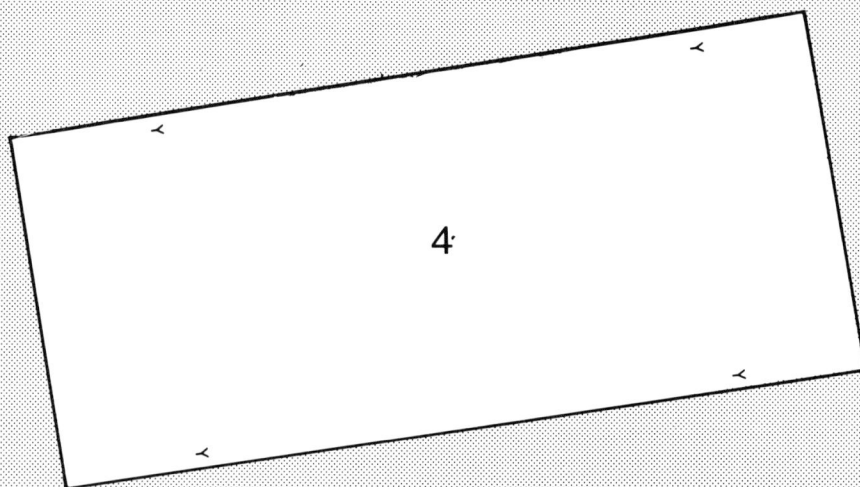

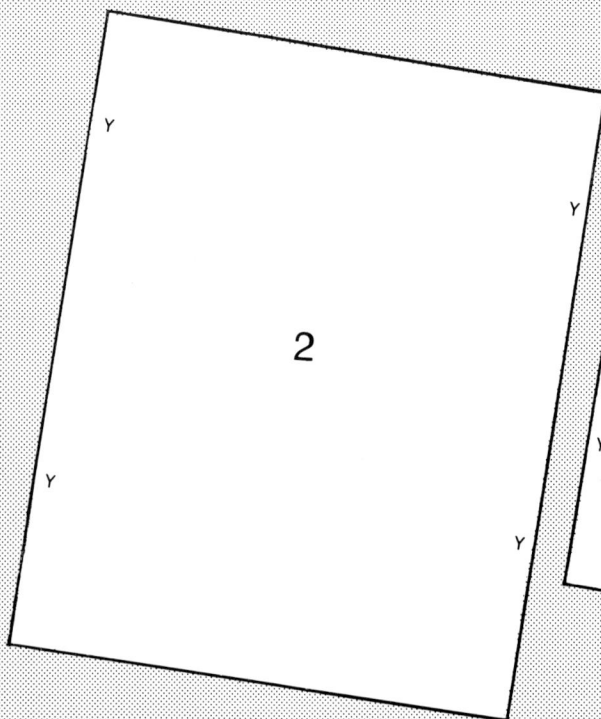

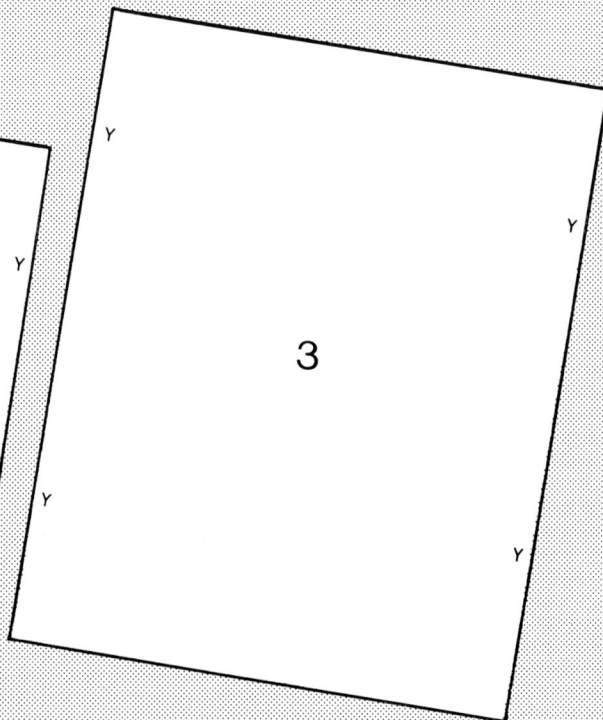

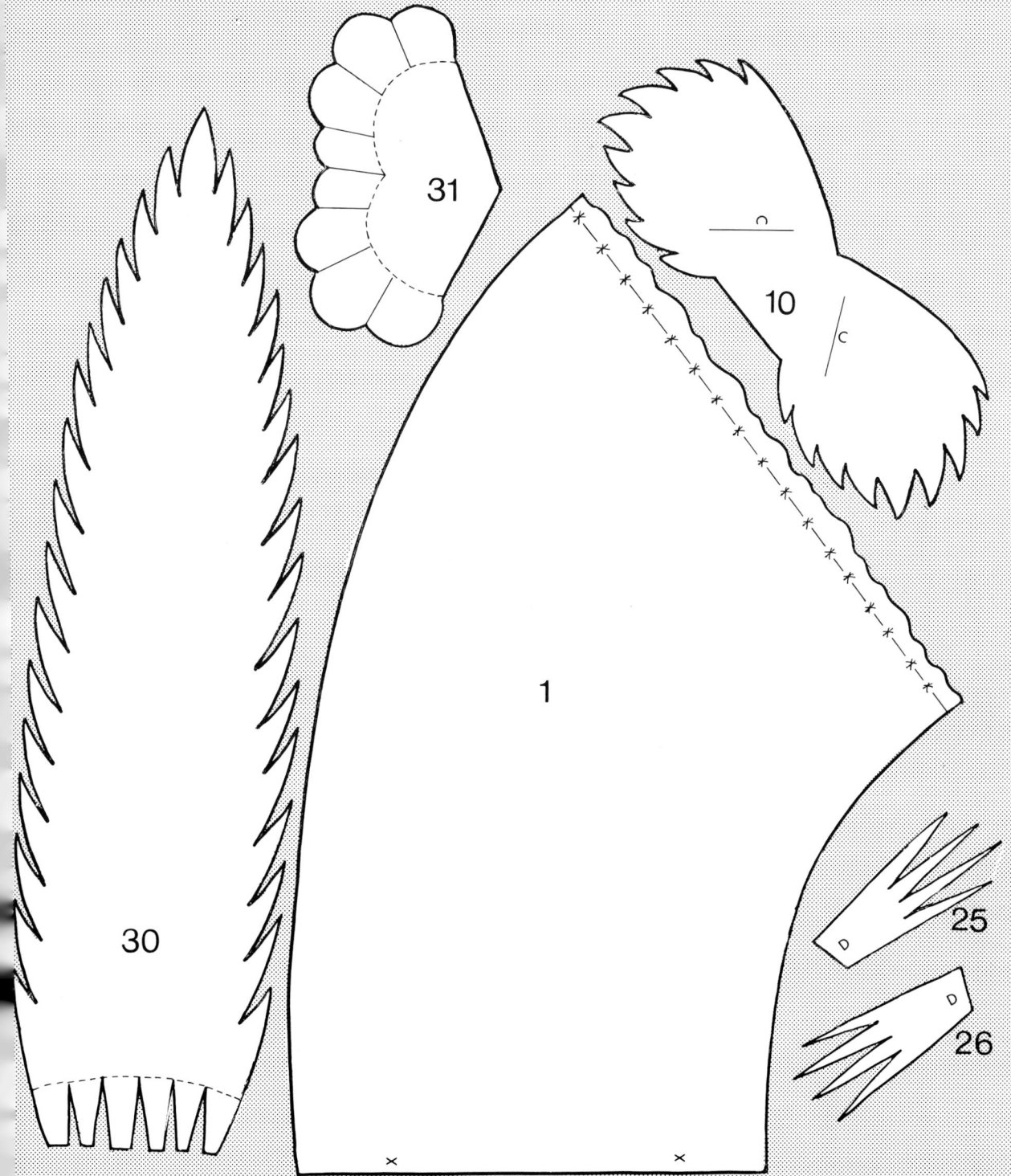

CAT UNITS

31

10

30

1

25

26

The Second King

As in the case of the Cat the diagrams for the Second King have been reduced considerably in size to get them into this book. The diagrams should be transferred to tracing paper and enlarged by the square-up process (see page 53).

The four units shown stippled are those for the microply armature on which the rest of the sculpture is built. There are in fact only three armature units, No. 38, the main body having been split towards the top to get it on to the page without too great a reduction in scale. The jagged edges indicated by the X arrows come together to make the complete armature, which should be of course cut from a single piece of ply. When the microply for the armature has been cut out it should be reinforced on the front with strips of balsa wood to stiffen it (Fig. 1).

Now take the main armature unit (38) and start to construct the sculpture. The Inner Collar (1) is attached first. In order to guard against possible cracking of the paper, it is advisable to give it curvature, before fixing, by drawing the collar between a straightedge and the glass cutting surface. Hold one end of the collar between finger and thumb and draw it gently under the straightedge. This 'biasing' treatment applies to all similarly curved units (see page 52).

After biasing, the Inner Collar is glued by tabs A behind the armature, so that the main part of the collar curves over the front of it (Fig. 2).

The Upper Leg (2) is biased and attached similarly, by tabs C, and the Boot Leg (3) attached likewise by tabs D (Fig. 2).

Next comes the Boot (4). Score along the lines a-a and b-b on the front side and fold back tabs C and D. Roll the front (right) part of the Boot over a 5 mm ($\frac{1}{5}$ in) dowel held behind the unit along the axis e-f, to give it a convex curvature. Glue the tab D over the edge of C. Looked at endways this creates a 'D' section with the curved part,

representing the toe area of the Boot, uppermost. Now roll the rear part of the Boot with the dowel along the axis g-h. This will form the curved back of the Boot. Slide the front end of the Boot over the armature and wrap the rear tab E behind, attaching with glue (Fig. 3).

Roll the Head (5) round a 5 mm ($\frac{1}{5}$ in) dowel along the axis A-B. Score along c-d, e-f, and g-h from the front. Score along d-e from behind. Bend tabs J, K and L back behind the head. Score along d-o from the front. Score along m-o from behind. Lift 'wing' of nostril along the score m-o. Bend 'nose' along score d-e so that it lies in the same plane as the armature.

Tabs J, K and L may now be glued behind the head area of the armature, taking care to establish the correct angles of top lip and chin by suitable adjustment of tabs K and L. The back of the Head at R is now bent behind the armature and glued. Tab N is now glued behind the armature to set the nose at the correct angle (Fig. 3).

Roll the Cap (6) into a conical form over a 1 cm ($\frac{1}{3}$ in) dowel and glue ends O and P behind armature (Fig. 4).

Roll Outer Collar (7) and attach over Inner Collar by gluing tabs B behind armature (Fig. 4).

Roll Shirt (8) and fix front (right) edge T armature. Glue a strip of balsa wood approximately $2\frac{1}{2} \times 10$ cm ($\frac{3}{4}$ in $\times$ 4 in) to front of armature about 3 cm (1 in) from right edge and glue left edge S of shirt to this (Fig. 4).

The Skirt (9) must first be scored in several places at front and rear. Scores a-b and c-d are on the front. Scores e-f and g-h are at the back. Scores u-v and j-k are on the front. Scores m-n and o-p are on the back; score q-r on the front and score s-t on the back. Bend all these scores to create a box-pleat effect (Fig. 4) and attach Skirt to right edge of armature by tab W bent behind. Arrange Skirt as shown in Fig. 4, mounting the left-hand tab X on a balsa wood strip approximately $2\frac{1}{2} \times 10$ cm ($\frac{3}{4}$ in × 4 in) glued to front of armature.

The Cloak is built up from Units 10, 11, 12 and 13. These are each biased with a straightedge into a convex curve on the long axis and their edges AA, BB, CC and DD brought together and glued. (Looked at endways each assume a teardrop profile.) Unit 10 is the left-hand fold of the Cloak, at the back of the figure. Unit 11 is glued on to this in the position shown in Fig. 5. Then Units 12 and 13 are added in such a way that the Cloak assumes the shape shown (Fig. 6).

Before fixing to the armature the upper part of the Cloak is then gently flattened a little by careful pressing between the palm of the hand and the working surface. The back of the left-hand part of 10 is then glued to the front surface of the left edge of the armature at Z. The right edge (Unit 13) of the Cloak is now propped about 1 cm ($\frac{1}{3}$ in) away from the surface of the Skirt with a distance-piece of balsa wood glued between it and the armature. The Belt (14) is now added by wrapping it round the front of the figure over the join between Shirt and Skirt. The Boot fringe (15) is fixed by biasing and fixing the tabs X and Y behind the armature (Fig. 7).

The Hair (16) is attached next. Before fixing, each hair strip is rolled from the bottom and secured in a single coil with a touch of glue (Fig. 7). When all the strips have been similarly coiled the Hair is attached by gluing along the back of the top edge and applying to the Head just where the Cap meets it. The front eyebrow area A is then bent behind the armature and attached (Fig. 7). The back area B is similarly wrapped round behind the Head and attached.

The Crown Spikes (17) are fixed by gluing along the back of the bottom edge and applying to the Hair at the angle shown in Fig. 7. Before fixing the tabs AA at each end of the Crown Spikes, the Inner Crown (18) must be made by punching the holes as indicated. The scalloped edge is made by 'nicking' it, also with the punch. The unit is then rolled into a cylindrical form and the tabs glued together at CC. The Inner Crown is then slipped over the cap and glued along the bottom edge at the point where the Crown Spikes are attached.

The tabs AA of the Crown Spikes are then glued behind the armature, taking care to preserve the inverted cone effect of the Crown Spikes.

Finally, the Crown Band (19) is added in the position shown in Fig. 7 and the ends BB attached behind the armature.

The Boot Top (20) is rolled into a cylindrical shape and attached at the top of the Boot by gluing the ends EE and fixing behind the armature (Fig. 7).

Now take the armature of the arm and attach the Hand (21) (the fingers of which should first be separated by cutting) by simply cementing it as a flat shape to the front surface F of the right-hand projection on the armature. The extreme end of the armature projection should lie just behind the roots of the fingers. The Forearm (22) is now rolled into a cylindrical form and the ends HH glued behind the armature at H.

The Upper Arm (23) is attached similarly at points KK (Fig. 8). The Upper Sleeve Support (24) is now attached by the tabs A and B (Fig. 9). The Upper Sleeve (25) is now prepared. Various scores are required. Those at a-a and b-b are on the front, while the other five, all marked s-s, are on the back. These scores are all folded forwards and the spaces between them are rolled over a 5 mm ($\frac{1}{5}$ in) dowel into convex curves. The end tabs G and H are then folded back and glued behind the armature (Fig. 10).

The arm is now glued on to the main body in the position shown (Fig. 11), using a small piece of balsa wood to act as distance-piece supporting the front part of the arm at the correct angle.

The Sole of the Boot (26) is fixed by a trace of glue along the bottom edge of the Boot and heel. The front end A is then wrapped round the front of the Boot and glued at the back of the armature. Similarly the back end B of the Sole is fixed behind the back end of the Boot (Fig. 11).

The Lip (27) is scored on the back and the upper and lower parts folded forwards slightly. A touch of glue is placed on the lip area of the Head. The lips are applied by tweezers (Fig. 11).

Tweezers are also used to fix the Eye (28). This is scored from the back and the upper (eyelash) part folded down. The iris is shaded in with a pencil or

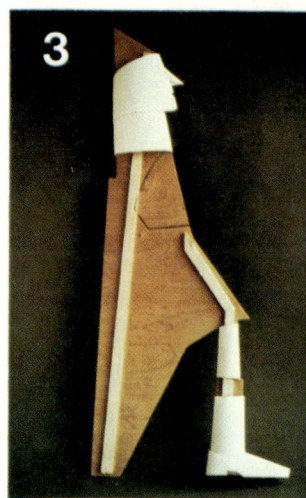

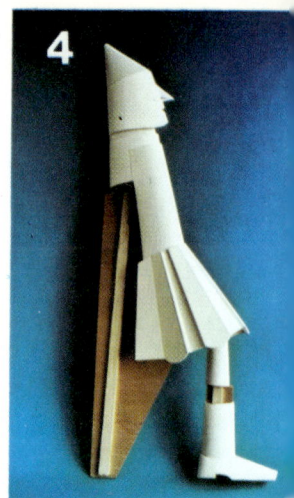

grey paint. Then the whole eye is fixed in place on the Head with tweezers and a touch of glue (Fig. 11).

The seven cuts in the Cuff (29) must be made before it is formed in a loop and glued along the tabs NN. It is then pulled gently between the forefingers of each hand to stretch the loop into an elongated oval. The inside of the tab area is now glued and the Cuff is threaded over the hand and fixed to the arm. (See photograph of completed figure.)

The Chalice is now made up on its armature. The Chalice Top (30) is rolled into a conical shape and attached by the ends PP to the back of the armature at its top PP. The Chalice Stem (31) is attached similarly at Q, followed by the Chalice Body (32). This is first formed into a cylinder and the ends R glued. The cylinder is then slipped over the armature, the edges of which have been previously glued.

The Chalice Base (33) is formed similarly and attached to the back of the upper part of the armature at S. Two identical decorative bands, (34) and (35), are formed into circles by gluing the tabs T together and attaching behind the armature at T. Before cutting these parts from the paper, the row of holes should be punched, using a pencil line on the back as a guide. The paper can then be cut to size on each side of the row of holes (this technique avoids any risk of the holes being torn).

The Knobs, (36) and (37), are fixed in place on the Cap top and the Chalice lid. These are slotted to a depth of about 3 mm ($\frac{1}{10}$ in) with the scalpel and the knobs inserted into the slots.

Finally, the Chalice is fixed in the correct position behind the Hand as shown in the photograph of the complete figure. A distance piece of balsa wood is introduced here to space the Chalice correctly behind the Hand. After the glue has set the fingers of the Hand can be curved to grip the Chalice base.

SECOND KING UNITS

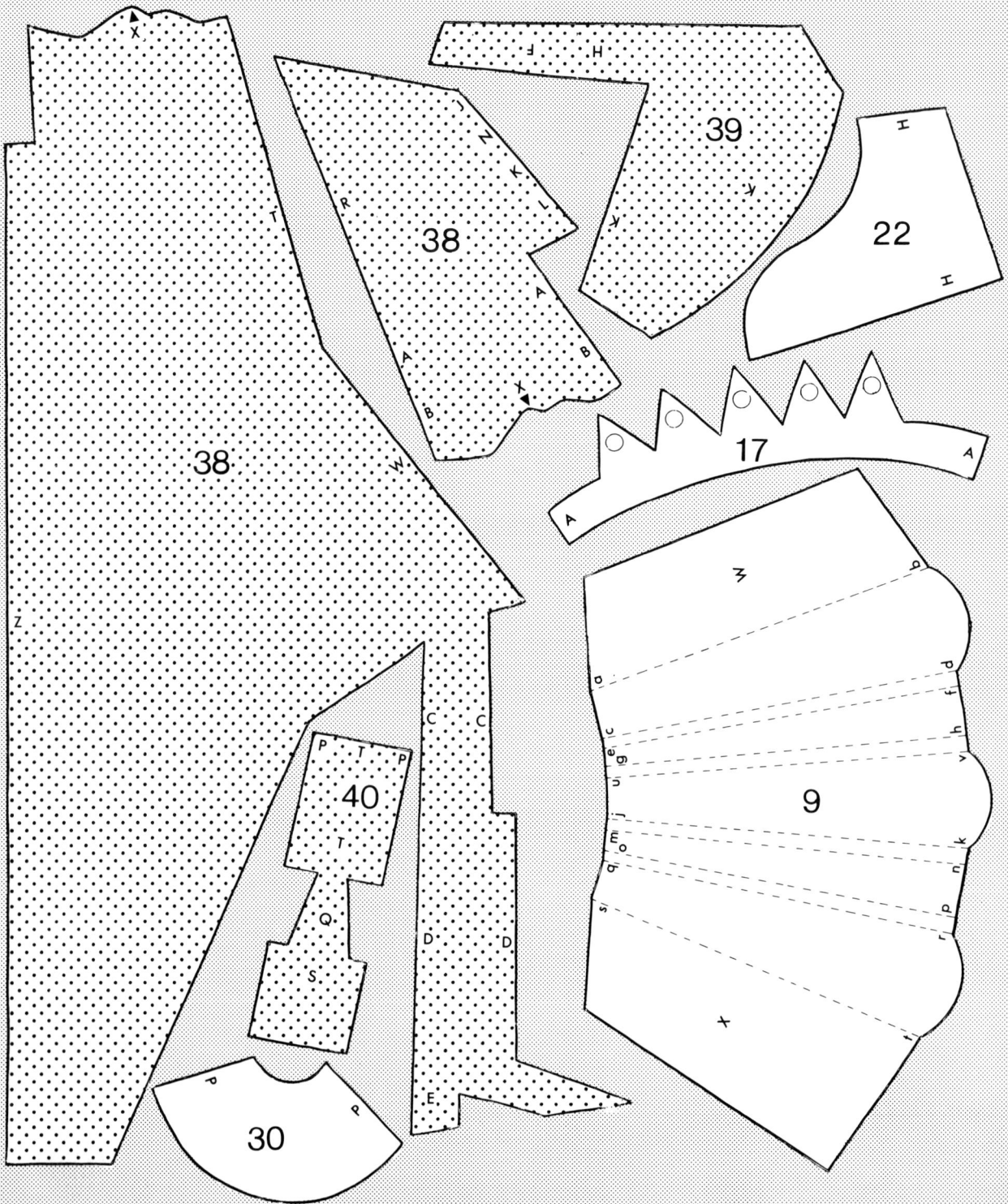

39

22

38

38

17

9

40

30

SECOND KING UNITS

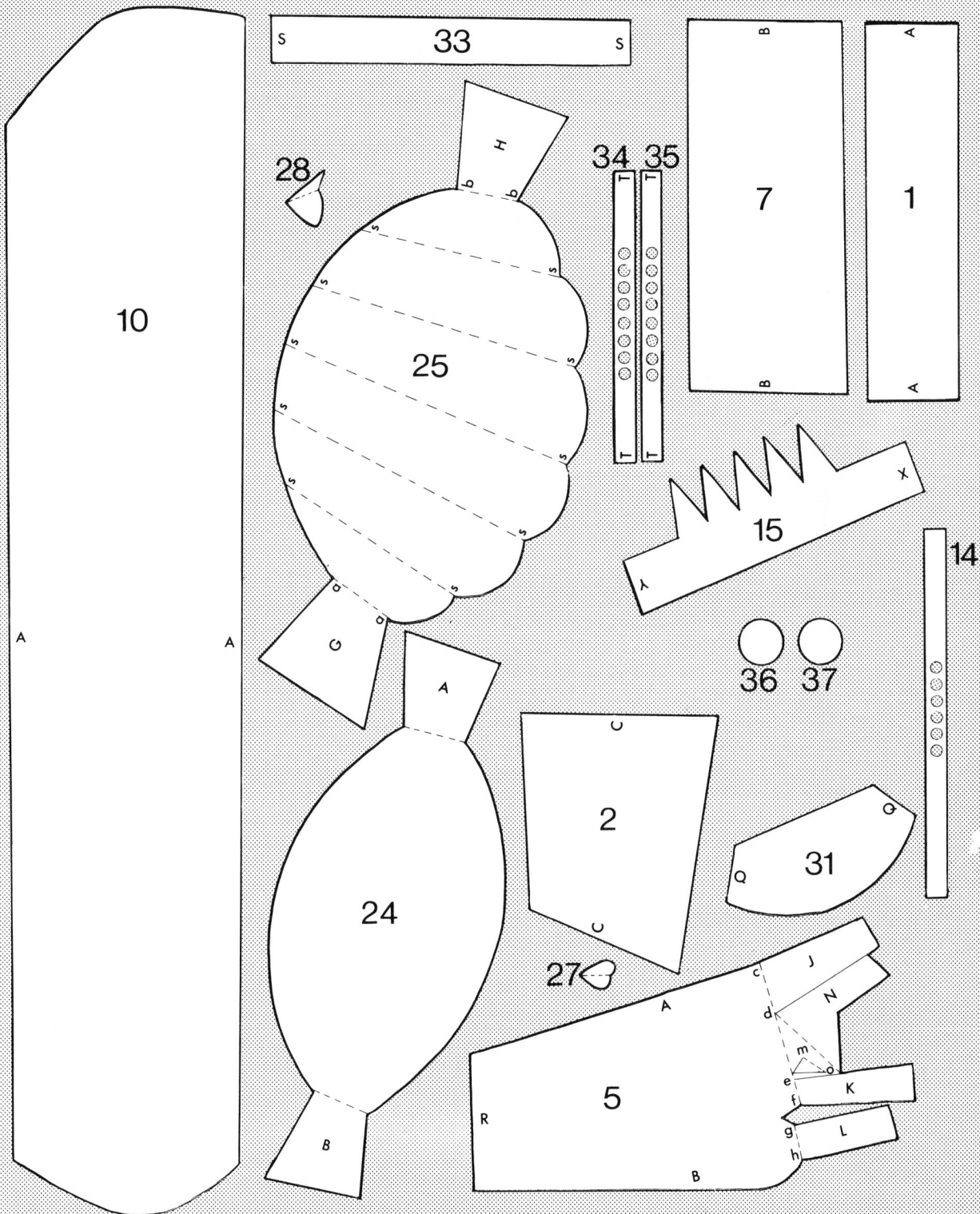

10

33
S   33   S

28

H

25

34 35
T T

7
B

B

1
A

A

15
X

Y

14

36 37

G

A

2
C

C

31
Q

Q

24

27

5
A

R

B

J

N

c

d

m

o

e

K

f

g

L

h

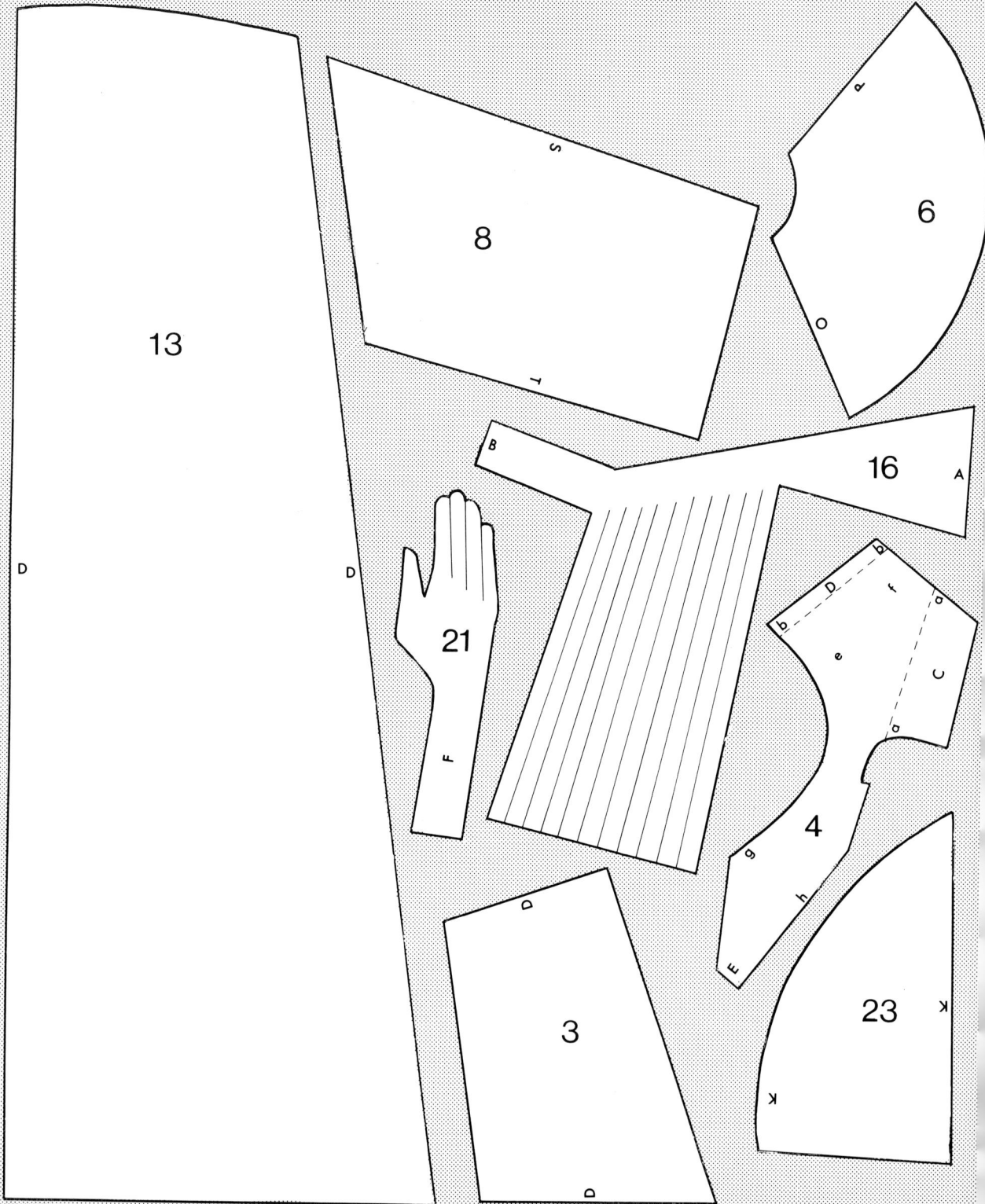

13

8

6

B 16 A

21

D D

b D f a
e C

4

g
h
E

3

D

D

23

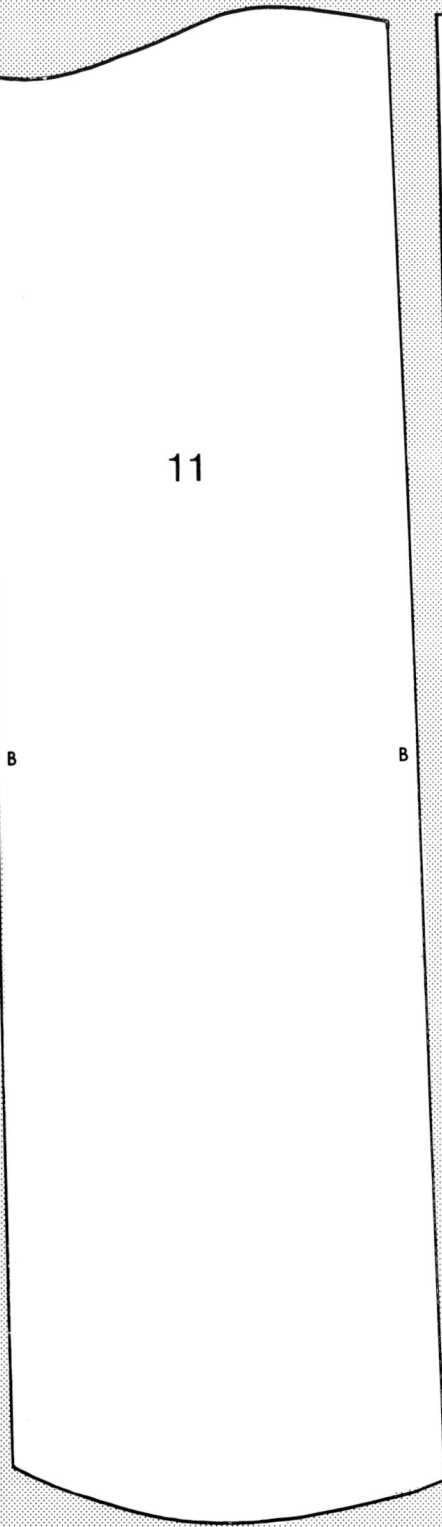

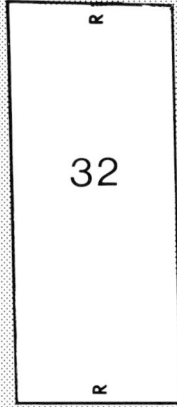

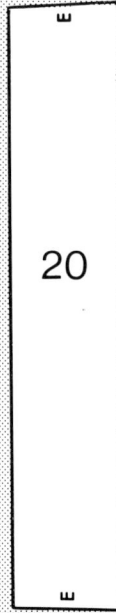

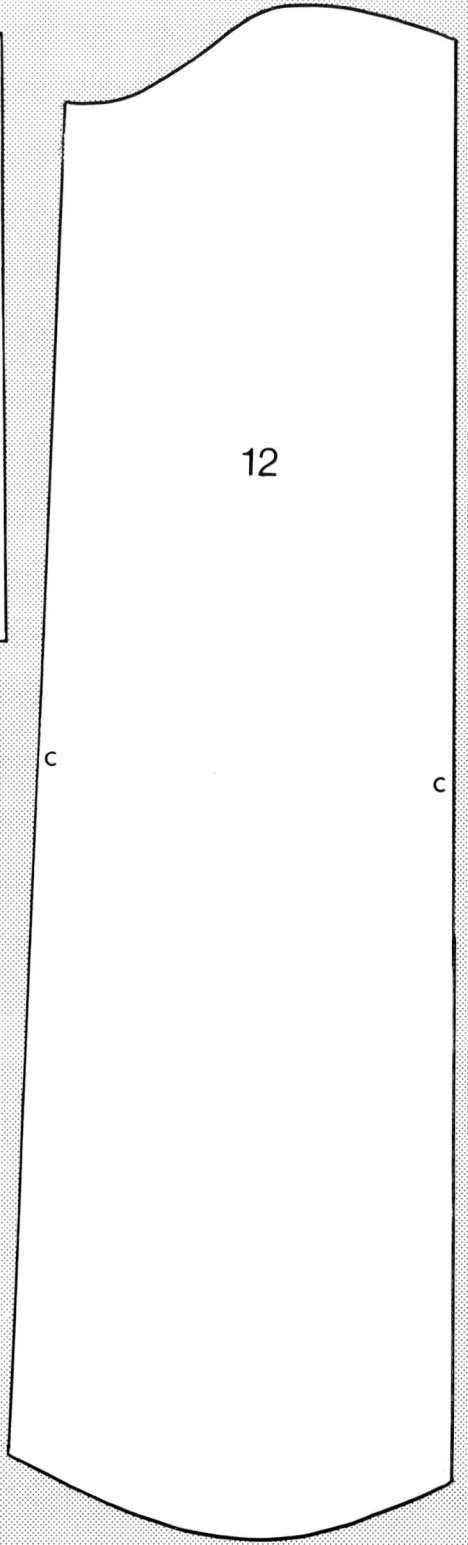

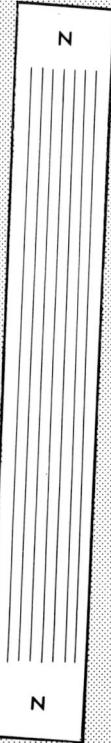

The Three Kings, for a Radio Times *Christmas cover and for a window display at Broadcasting House*

Framing

The only difference between framing a water-colour, oil painting or photograph and framing a paper sculpture is in the space needed to accommodate the sculpture between the glass and the back panel. Any picture frame which appeals to you and which is about the right size for your purpose can be adapted to take a paper sculpture. All that is needed is extra timber, about 1 cm ($\frac{1}{3}$ in) thick and wide enough for the purpose. With accurate use of the tenon saw this can easily be cut into four sections to form a box of the correct size to fit fairly tightly into the rebate behind the frame. The box will also serve the purpose of holding the glass in place. Mitred joints at the corners of the box are neatest and not beyond the skill of anyone capable of making a paper sculpture. A mitre-block, vice and tenon saw are all that is needed (together with the usual Bostik or Uhu and a few thin panel pins to help hold the corners together). Butt joints, however, if neatly made, are quite adequate for the purpose.

The box can be glued into the rebate of the picture frame, or held in place by a fillet of wood about 7 mm ($\frac{1}{4}$ in) square in section, surrounding the box and attached to the back of the frame. Small screws can then hold the box in place, making it easier to change the glass if it gets damaged.

The back panel, on to which the sculpture is mounted, should fit over the back of the box, but be slightly smaller so that it does not show from the front. The back panel can then be screwed on to the box after the paper sculpture has been fixed to it.

Internal lining to the box is important. It can simply be painted with poster or other colour of the correct shade to set off the sculpture, but the addition of some kind of texture, as a contrast to the paper of the sculpture, can enrich its effect. All kinds of materials can be used, such as velvet, flock paper, or hessian.

When I held my exhibition at Reed House in the mid-60s, I was suddenly confronted with the necessity of framing about 50 sculptures, from the large Wren poster to the small Little Mermaid and Gendarme. An exhibition contractor made all these frames for me, but the principles upon which they were constructed are quite simple and within the scope of anyone handy with a saw. Glass of the right size should be obtained first, then the basic box, comprising the sides of the frame, made up. Mitre joints were used by the contractor but butt

Below *The Bruce Angrave paper sculpture exhibition at Reed House, Piccadilly, London*

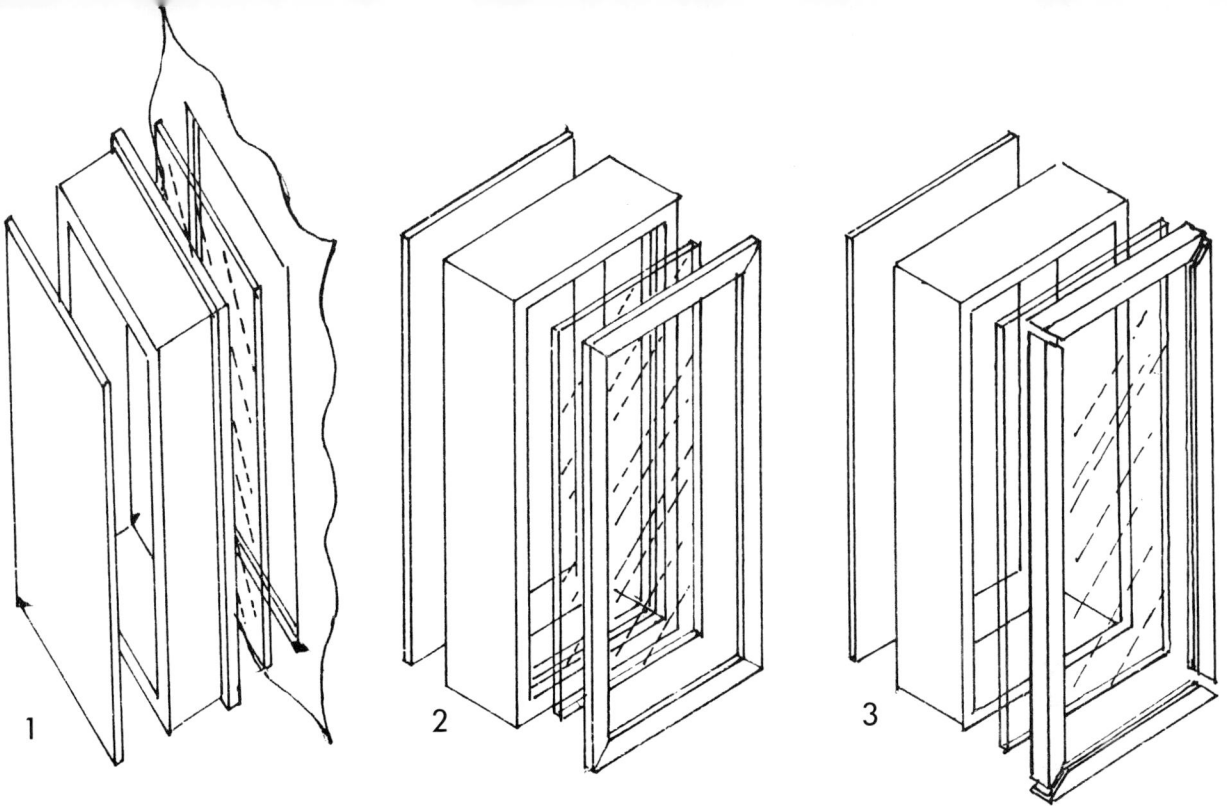

1 *Deep frame built on to existing picture frame.* 2 *Purpose-built deep frame resembling those used in Reed House exhibition.* 3 *Simple type of purpose-built deep frame*

joints are adequate. Around the inside edge of the front of the box a moulding of wood about $\frac{1}{2}$ cm ($\frac{1}{5}$ in) square section is then attached with pins and glue. This is set back from the front edge to the depth of the thickness of the glass. The glass is then inserted. Another moulding of wood, about $\frac{1}{2}$ cm ($\frac{1}{5}$ in) thick and of a width sufficient to hold the glass in place, is then added on the front. It is important that this moulding should have mitred corners. The box frame is then complete. All that needs to be added is the back panel, attached as described above.

Another, even simpler, type of box frame, utilises L sections of wood moulding. With this type of frame the glass is cut to the same size as the box and lies on its front surface. The L-shaped mouldings (with mitred corners) overlap the box with one of the arms of the L, while the other acts as the front of the frame, holding the glass in place at the same time.

Framing full-round sculpture is more complicated. In this case a box made of transparent material is required, with a solid (wood) back or base. My Roman Chariot is framed in a professionally made perspex box, but these (as with anything professionally, or for that matter, unprofessionally, made nowadays) are expensive. This particular box cost £45 in 1979, not including the back panel. I have never tried to construct my own perspex box but doubtless this is possible, using the special perspex cements which are available. The panels of perspex (themselves quite expensive) would have to be cut very accurately, and the cut edges polished before cementing, to give a professional finish.

Preserving

A paper sculpture in an airtight frame will be quite safe from deterioration. Like any framed painting, it is best not kept in bright light, as some papers tend to yellow with time and if it is painted the colours tend to fade. Various surface preservatives are on the market. These come in aerosols such as Letracote Matt, which by simple spraying covers the paper with an invisible protective film.

Lighting

Correct lighting is most important. If a framed sculpture is hung directly opposite a window, for example, not only will the modelling be 'flattened' but also reflections in the glass will be a nuisance.

Most of my sculptures are designed to be lighted from a particular angle and I try to hang them near windows giving light from the same direction. Artificial lighting can be effectively placed with spotlights mounted on the ceiling or opposite wall. Occasionally, built-in internal lighting is a good solution. Short fluorescent tubes can be bought which are excellent for this. Concealed behind a sufficiently wide frame they give a diffuse light which does not cast harsh shadows. These lamps, too, unlike tungsten lamps, run at a fairly low temperature and so do not overheat the air inside the frame.

Below *Future City, for a magazine illustration*

Photography

For several years I photographed my paper sculptures on a quarter- or half-plate camera with studio tripod, using various professional photographic tungsten lights plus arc lights. These last had the characteristic of emitting very sharp polarised beams of light. When focused through a suitable lens, they could add crisp brilliant highlights which, combined with the softer lighting of the tungsten lamps, emphasised the three-dimensional quality of the sculptures. This elaborate photographic equipment was part of my father's studio and even then was expensive to acquire. Today it would be prohibitive. Fortunately, modern small cameras have improved so much in recent years that it is no longer necessary to go to such lengths. Most of my present photography is done either with a 35 mm single-lens reflex or with a 6 cm square twin-lens Yashicamat. My latest 35 mm camera, a Canon AE1, is fully automatic and estimates its exposures with great accuracy. When using the twin-lens reflex (or for that matter any other non-automatic camera) I use an exposure meter.

Very occasionally, when photographing a paper sculpture which is to be reproduced on a very large scale, for example a poster, I still use an antique mahogany and brass half-plate studio camera equipped with a modern anastigmat lens. But then I was lucky to buy it some years ago for £5. Now like everything else these fine old cameras have all been 'collected' and are unobtainable. With this camera I use modern portable lights with photoflood lamps, combined with reflectors of white card which soften the light and illumine the shadows. In the case of the recent Letraset 'International City' commission I used, in addition, six or seven ordinary household tungsten lamps interspersed between and behind the 'buildings'. These gave a glowing effect unobtainable by other means.

Cast shadows are to be avoided in paper sculpture photography as they add confusing shapes and obscure modelling. For this reason I try to use daylight whenever possible. Outdoor lighting on a bright but not brilliantly sunny day is best for this, but although absence of sun makes England an excellent place for such photography it is often difficult to deal with background problems. When I had my ninth-floor flat near Baker Street I could arrange sculptures on the terrace-balcony so that I had an open sky behind, but in my present garden this isn't possible. I sometimes use large sheets of paper or cloth supported on wood frames but this can only be done when wind is totally absent.

At other times with small sculptures I find my fifth-floor studio attic windows are excellent when the light is bright but not too sunny. A diffuse soft light is directed from the window side and the dark areas of the sculpture are illumined with white card reflectors, or if more reflected light is needed, with reflectors made of crumpled and then straightened-out kitchen foil.

Strangely enough, it is much easier to photograph white paper sculptures in colour than in black-and-white. This is because the colour of the light, and its complementary colour in the shadows, adds an extra dimension of interest. Suitably coloured backgrounds and foregrounds also can enhance the effect of the sculpture. I find that the truest effects are achieved with colour transparencies rather than prints. Both 35 mm and 6 cm square colour slides can be seen very brilliantly through an eye-level battery-powered viewer. More sophisticated table viewers are semi-automatic and can take a dozen or so transparencies at a time, transporting them one by one through the viewer by means of a hand-operated slider. The most sophisticated table viewers have a translucent screen upon which the transparencies are projected via a reflector from a mains-operated quartz-iodine lamp. Several people can thus view the transparencies at the same time.

Then there are the large-screen projectors, hand-operated, semi- or fully-automatic. With these the transparencies can be thrown on to a screen of considerable size, the disadvantage being that a darkened room is needed for best effect.

With all mains-driven projectors the quartz-iodine lamp is preferable as it gives a much brighter, very white light which does not darken with use, as is the case with the older tungsten lamps.

Stereo photography seems somewhat mindlessly to have gone out of fashion in recent years. I still possess and use a 25-year-old battery-driven stereo viewer with focusing and eye-width adjustment. This takes 35 mm stereo slides but is, I am told, no longer obtainable. The firm of Duval, 217 High Road, London W4, specialise in stereo equipment and tell me that a stereo camera using a 120 rollfilm, called the Iso Duplex, is still made and that stereo daylight viewers can be obtained through them.

Paper sculpture is a particularly suitable subject for stereo photography, as its three-dimensional quality is brought out with startling vividness by this means. I do not use a purpose-made stereo camera myself, but instead possess an ingenious and simple device which fits on top of the tripod and can shift a normal 35 mm camera from side to side so that two separate frames, one for each eye, can be taken and subsequently mounted in a stereo slide. A secondhand camera shop might, who knows, still occasionally be able to supply some of this old ingenious stereo equipment. So might the pages of *Exchange and Mart*. There is no harm in trying!

Flashguns are quite unsuitable for the photography of paper sculpture, unless sophisticated apparatus using equipment mounted on stands away from the sculpture is used. Even then this method is unsatisfactory as the quality of the lighting cannot be judged visually before the

Above *The Photographer, for a fashion display*
Opposite *The Penguin*

photograph is taken. Camera-mounted flashguns are worst of all as they give flat front lighting which irons out all modelling. On only one occasion have I used a camera-mounted flashgun—at the Ministry of the Environment stand at the Ideal Home Exhibition some years ago. This was simply because there was no other way of getting any kind of record. As the sculptures were in colour the flattening effect was not wholly disastrous, but reflections of the flash were only too obvious in the slightly sheened surface of the photographically enlarged background drawings.

The Policeman